TROPICAL
FRESHWATER AQUARIA

The hobby of keeping tropical fish has much to recommend it. Tropical fish are clean, do not smell, do not need letting out early morning and late at night and can be left alone for up to three weeks while their owner is away on vacation. The well-kept community tank is also a decorative feature which is an asset to any home.

This book is a short guide written to help the beginner avoid those elementary mistakes which can so easily occur and which can be very discouraging. However, we have attempted to deal with the subject in a scientific manner, to provide a background for understanding the biology of tropical fish and to serve as an introduction for further reading. In the study of tropical fish, there are still more questions unanswered than facts known, so even novice aquarists with time, interest and patience can make completely new observations and valuable contributions to our biological knowledge.

We would like to thank the curators of various aquaria throughout the world for their assistance with this book.

G.C. & P.B.

A
GROSSET
ALL-COLOR GUIDE

TROPICAL FRESHWATER AQUARIA

BY GEORGE CUST AND PETER BIRD
Illustrated by George Thompson

GROSSET & DUNLAP
A NATIONAL GENERAL COMPANY
Publishers • New York

590.7

THE GROSSET ALL-COLOR GUIDE SERIES
SUPERVISING EDITOR . . . GEORG ZAPPLER

CONTENTS

4 **Introduction**

8 **The aquarium**
20 Aquarium equipment
28 Contents of the aquarium

43 **The fish**
50 Family Poeciliidae
64 Family Cyprinodontidae
70 Family Cyprinidae
82 Family Anabantidae
90 Family Characidae
104 Family Cichlidae

120 **Foods and feeding**
126 Foods for fry

128 **Diseases of fish**

138 **Setting up the
home aquarium**

156 **Books to read**

157 **Index**

INTRODUCTION

An aquarium, from the Latin, *aqua* meaning water, is defined by the dictionary as, 'an artificial pool or tank for the keeping of live aquatic plants and animals. A place of public entertainment containing tanks'. We will, in this book, think of an aquarium as any container capable of holding water, fish and/or plants and being inside a building. This does not include artificial or natural ponds outside. Places of public exhibition will be called Aquaria with a capital letter.

The keeping of aquaria has a long history. In 1596, Chang Ch'en-te wrote a book describing how he kept goldfish in tanks. Samuel Pepys wrote in his diary of 1665 (Lord's Day), 'My wife and I shown a fine rarity: of fishes kept in a glass of water, that will live for ever; and finely marked they are being foreign'. As early as 1853 the world's first public Aquarium was built at the London Zoological Gardens. In 1868, M. Simon, the French Consul at Ningpo, brought from China to Paris some Paradise-fish *(Macropodus opercularis)* and gave them to Pierre Corbonnier. Later these fish spawned in an aquarium.

In the Far East, young fish are introduced into rice paddies when the rice is planted. Later fish and rice are harvested together.

Triumphant young Amazon Indian with Pacu fish. The Pacu (*Colossoma* sp) is a rarely imported aquarium fish from northern South America. In the wild it feeds mainly on fruit.

Today several hundred species of tropical fish are kept and bred in the home aquarium. Rare species are frequently imported, and selective breeding and cross breeding have resulted in the improvement (though sometimes the worsening) of strains and the development of many varieties to add color to the home aquarium.

There is another aspect of tropical fish which is perhaps not realized by most aquarists. In their native areas, these fish provide food for many people. They are hunted in a variety of ways—by spear, poisons, fish traps and different types of nets. Another increasing way of providing fish for food is by fish farming; a number of species, particularly of the genus *Tilapia,* are being farmed. One way in which this is done is by putting young fish in rice paddies when the rice is planted. Later, fish measuring five inches or more are harvested with the rice.

Public Aquaria

Public Aquaria throughout the world have an obvious advantage over the home aquarist in that they afford the space to keep many larger and more exotic specimens of tropical fish. Cichlid fish, for instance, are displayed to the best effect in vast tanks such as the New York Aquarium at Coney Island and Steinhart Aquarium in San Francisco. In addition to the aesthetic and entertainment value of these places, the fish they keep are frequently of scientific interest.

In public Aquaria a great deal of thought has to be given to displaying the fish to their best advantage. Many exhibit them in brightly lit tanks within a darkened room. Under such circumstances great detail can be observed both at the front and the back of the tanks, and the eye is not distracted by surrounding decor. The fish are usually divided into three main sections: cold freshwater fish, seawater fish and tropical freshwater fish.

The services of all public Aquaria are large. There must, for instance, be reserve tanks for new arrivals to be quarantined and acclimatizing tanks for the treatment of diseased fish. Most Aquaria have a small breeding section to reproduce the more easily bred fish. Many have complex systems of water

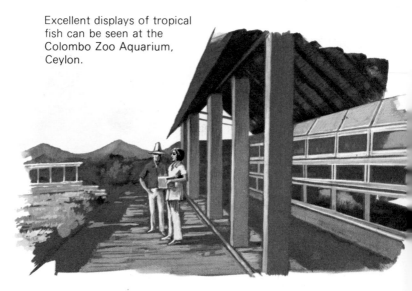

Excellent displays of tropical fish can be seen at the Colombo Zoo Aquarium, Ceylon.

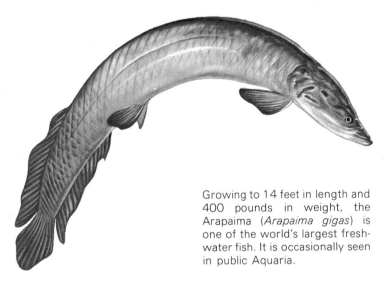

Growing to 14 feet in length and 400 pounds in weight, the Arapaima (*Arapaima gigas*) is one of the world's largest freshwater fish. It is occasionally seen in public Aquaria.

filtration and aeration. At some Aquaria special tanks constructed of fiberglas are shaped to give an impression of no corners and a greater perspective is achieved. Aquaria in tropical countries are particularly fortunate in having easily available supplies of tropical fish, and they usually exhibit first-class displays.

The attractive Giant Gourami (*Colisa fasciata*) is popular in many public Aquaria. Gouramis are distinguished by their thread-like ventral fins, used as tactile organs.

7

THE AQUARIUM

Factors in selection

When purchasing an aquarium there are two main factors to be considered: size, which will be determined by the dimensions of the intended site, and weight, a factor which is frequently overlooked. The smaller 14-inch × 8-inch × 8-inch tank presents no problems, but the larger tanks certainly do. A full 24-inch × 12-inch × 12-inch tank will weigh approximately 100 pounds and will, therefore, require adequate support. Any flat surface can quite easily be used to hold a fish tank, but it is sometimes preferable to use a stand, of which many kinds are available.

Most of the standard-sized tanks can be purchased with a matching stand strong enough to bear the weight, but as the legs often have no feet, extra covering on floors may be required in order to distribute the load. Metal stands are made in one, two or three tiers, and if a unit of three 24-inch × 12-inch × 12-inch tanks is installed, the approximate total weight is around 400 pounds. It is therefore imperative that the unit is placed on a strong, if not solid, floor. It is always a good idea to purchase a two- or three-tier stand even if initially only one tank is purchased. The spare levels can be covered and used temporarily for storage space.

The weight of a full aquarium must be considered before purchase. As a guide, one cubic foot of water weighs 62 pounds.

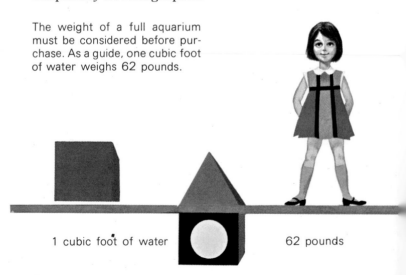

1 cubic foot of water   62 pounds

Slotted steel angle frames

A decorative stand incorporating a slotted steel angle frame can be readily assembled.

If the intending aquarist is an eager 'do-it-yourself' man, he may wish to build a special unit using timber and masonite, etc. to fit exactly into a specific space in a room. Care must be taken to make the main frame of sufficient thickness, remembering that if the cross members warp with the weight, a leaking tank may result. Another point to remember with this type of unit is the adequate provision for servicing both on

An attractive bow-fronted tank with a wrought iron stand.

the surface of the water and between the individual tanks. An ideal material for a special framework is slotted steel angle. This can be made up into virtually any size and shape and clad in a suitable material to finish it off. It is also easily dismantled for moving or decorating.

Although the waters of the earth vary considerably in temperature, an aquarium is usually classified as either tropical or cold. Normally this means that cold water aquaria adjust their temperature to their surroundings, whereas the temperature of tropical aquaria is maintained artifically. Our native fish have to withstand a temperature range from just above freezing (32° F) to 60°-65° F. Fish from the tropics experience a much smaller yearly range, in some cases only one or two degrees, and the tropical aquarium is kept at 75° F with only minor variations all the year round. There are, of course, fish that live in intermediate temperature ranges, and these can be adapted quite easily one way or the other provided extremes are not attempted.

The vast majority of private aquaria in this country are freshwater but with continual advance in techniques, marine aquaria are becoming more widespread. Many individual homes contain tropical fish tanks or aquaria simply for decorative purposes. The cheapness and availability of materials and equipment in recent years has greatly

Aquascapes, one type of aquarium, display bog plants and fish in shallow water.

increased their popularity. Tanks adorn corners and recesses, fill holes in walls and can even act as a divider in a large room.

It is also believed that the presence of tropical fish tanks can have a therapeutic effect. For this reason many public offices and doctors' and dentists' waiting rooms have them installed. Undoubtedly, the peaceful and attractive color of a well-kept tank do have a restful effect on the human mind.

The majestic *Pterois volitans,* one of the marine scorpion fish.

Angle iron tank

Tank with typical hood

All-plastic tank

Tank frame ready for glazing

Aquarium design

As rectangular tanks are the most satisfactory, their development in recent years has taken many forms. The frame is usually of angle iron to provide the necessary strength and rigidity, although the smaller tanks can safely use pressed steel. This type of tank, although the most commonly used, has the disadvantage of rusting easily around the top of the metal frame. To avoid this problem quite a number of alternative methods of construction have been employed.

Tanks molded completely in glass are available from dealers in varying sizes, usually up to 15 inches $\times$ 10 inches $\times$ 10 inches. Care must be taken with these, however, as one knock on a corner when moving usually means disaster. Larger molded glass tanks are even more difficult to handle but are less likely to break if placed on a sheet of felt or cardboard. A disadvantage with tanks of this construction is that one's vision is often distorted because the thickness of the glass is not uniform. This is because the tanks are cast in one piece and the mold is not of the same thickness throughout.

For some years there has been on the market a tank made completely of plastic. It is not molded from one piece but consists of flat sheets of clear and colored plexiglass cemented together. Because of the flexible nature of the plexiglass, these tanks cannot be made very large and in time the front often becomes scratched.

More recently, an enterprising manufacturer has produced tanks of various sizes using fiberglas for the frame and base. Regular glass is used for the front, back and sides. These appear to have many advantages: the fiberglas is hard, can be produced in a variety of colors, and is non-corrosive. Another recent development, which has just been commercialized, is the sealing of angle iron frames by coating them with a layer of hard plastic before glazing. Some ingenious aquarists restricted by finance have made tank frames from wood, but this method is to be recommended only to the carpenter with years of experience.

With so many types of tanks to choose from, cost is bound to have an effect on the final decision. The metal-framed tanks are usually the least expensive in the range and the chromium-plated and fiberglas types are more expensive.

The dimensions of the aquarium have an important bearing on the number and health of the fish it contains. During life, like all animals, fish take in oxygen (O_2) and give out carbon dioxide (CO_2). This process is called respiration. Dissolved oxygen is extracted from the water, and carbon dioxide, a waste product from the fish, is released in the water and finally escapes into the air. The amount of oxygen never becomes critical except under very unusual circumstances, but a high level of carbon dioxide can be poisonous to the fish. This may happen when there are too many fish in too small a tank, each fish producing its own quota of carbon dioxide. As this CO_2 cannot escape quickly enough, it accumulates in the water, eventually killing the fish.

A tank with a small surface area, such as the typical goldfish bowl, through which less carbon dioxide can escape, is obviously potentially more harmful than one with the same volume of water but a large surface area and shallow depth.

Plants in sunlight give off oxygen and absorb carbon dioxide so that when the aquarium is lit this helps to reduce the amount of carbon dioxide present. This process, however, is reversed during the hours of darkness. Aeration by disturbing the surface of the water helps carbon dioxide to leave the water more easily, especially in an overcrowded tank.

The gill is the site of gaseous exchange in the fish.

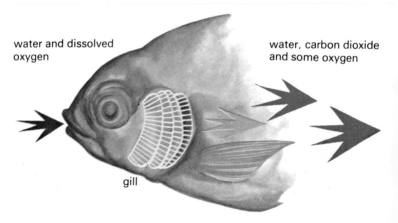

water and dissolved oxygen

water, carbon dioxide and some oxygen

gill

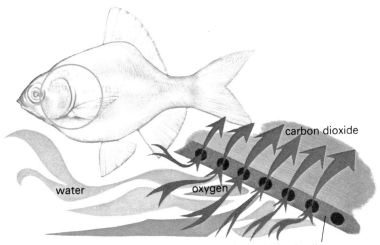

carbon dioxide

water   oxygen

blood capillary with red blood cells

In the gill, thin-walled capillaries are exposed to a flow of water from the mouth. Oxygen is absorbed from the water and carbon dioxide given up.

We have stressed the importance of carbon dioxide accumulation and not oxygen deficiency in all of these instances. Oxygen shortage occurs very rarely, only in those conditions of severe organic pollution of a tank by overfeeding of dry foods or of *Daphnia*, which have subsequently died. The rotting of this food by millions of bacteria and protozoa makes considerable biological demands on the oxygen supply.

A large surface area relative to depth is necessary for efficient gaseous exchange. Fish are often seen gasping in goldfish bowls with small surface areas.

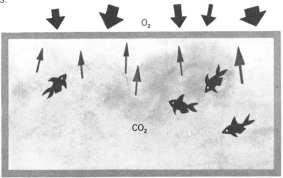

Water

The water cycle

The continuous process of exchange of water between the land, sea and atmosphere is called the water cycle. Water vapor gets into the air by evaporation from the oceans and, to a lesser extent, from lakes and rivers. Vegetation also gives off large amounts of water vapor to the atmosphere by transpiration from leaves. The supply is drawn from soil moisture by the root system of the plants.

Rain water is formed when water vapor condenses in the atmosphere. This occurs when the water vapor in the air is cooled, either because it is forced to rise or for other reasons. The total precipitation, including snow, frost, hail, etc. eventually finds its way back by rivers and streams to the sea, or it may end up temporarily in a lake.

The water cycle in the earth-atmosphere system. Taps indicate sources of domestic water supply.

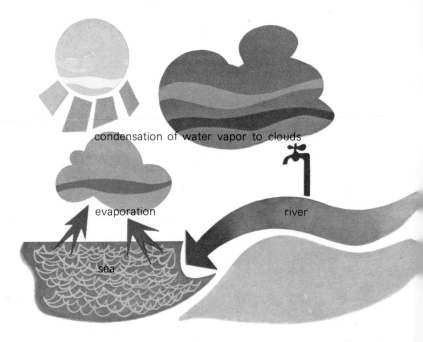

condensation of water vapor to clouds

evaporation

river

sea

No surface water is completely pure; soot, hydrocarbons and sulphur dioxide (expecially in large cities) chemicals in soil and rocks, and sewage effluent encountered on its course can be absorbed by the rain water. The taps in the schematic representation of the water cycle below indicate the stages in the cycle at which the domestic water supply is taken. The mineral constituents of river, reservoir and water from underground strata are seldom injurious to health. Such water is readily made available for human consumption by treatment to eliminate all disease-producing bacteria. Purification is accomplished by mechanical filtering out of bacteria followed by their destruction by other organisms and, finally, by chemical oxidation.

The cycle is completed when the surface water is reabsorbed into the atmosphere and the process begins again.

upland reservoir

rain

water in underground strata

The hardness of water

Pure rain water, distilled water or demineralized water contain no other chemicals. Once rain water passes through the ground, however, it dissolves the minerals contained therein.

One of the most common minerals is limestone (calcium carbonate, $CaCO_3$) and water containing excess amounts is said to be hard (temporary hardness). Other salts which make water hard are magnesium salts (permanent hardness). One of the common characteristics of hard water is that soaps lather very poorly. To the aquarist a knowledge of water types is important because fish and plants thrive best where the degree of hardness is at the optimum level for the species concerned. The Neon Tetra *(Hyphessobrycon innesi)* for example, is at its best in soft water, whereas the Celebes Sailfin *(Telmatherina ladigesi)* prefers hard water. Hardness is therefore determined by the amount of $CaCO_3$ present in the water and this can be expressed in any of the three following ways:

(1) parts per million of $CaCO_3$ (ppm);
(2) grains of $CaCO_3$ per gallon (Clark degrees);
(3) parts of $CaCO_3$ per 100,000 (German degree DH).

Different books use different scales and it is useful to remember that 1 Clark degree equals 14 ppm or 4/5 DH.

Water description	ppm	° DH	° Clark
Soft	0–50	0–5	0–3.5
Medium	50–150	5–15	3.5–10.5
Hard	150–300	15–30	10.5–21.0
Very Hard	Over 300	Over 30	Over 21

Examples of fish which thrive best in soft water include the Discus *(Symphysodon discus)* and *Pterophyllum* and *Aphyosemion* species, while the Celebes Sailfin *(Telmatherina ladigesi)*, *Bedotia geayi* and *Tanichthys albonubes* prefer water of medium hardness. The Platy *(Xiphophorus maculatus)* and the Sailfin Molly *(Mollienesia latipinna)*, on the other hand, require considerably harder water. It is difficult to be as specific about the requirements of plants. Like fish, some have wide tolerances; for example, the cryptocorynes will flourish in virtually any fresh water.

The pH *value of water*

The *p*H value of a solution is a number used to express its acidity or alkalinity and is an expression of the total number of hydrogen ions in the solution. Neutral water has a *p*H of 7, therefore water with a *p*H less than 7 has an acid reaction and water with a *p*H greater than 7 is alkaline. This scale is logarithmic so that water with a *p*H of 6 has a concentration of hydrogen ions ten times that of water with a *p*H of 7.

In nature the alkalinity of water is usually determined by its calcium carbonate and bicarbonate content. This is also responsible for hardness. Although *p*H and hardness are separate factors in nature, hard water is nearly always alkaline. Acid water in nature is usually due to the presence of peat or decaying vegetation, conditions which tend to make water soft.

The acidity or alkalinity of water may be measured by using dyes which change color according to changes in *p*H. For example, one drop of the B.D.H. Universal Indicator dye plus one drop of water is green at *p*H 7, blue at *p*H 8, orange at *p*H 6, etc. Such dyes are available as *p*H kits from pet shops.

Colors obtained from indicator dyes provide an estimate of *p*H.

0   1   2   3   4   5   6   7   8   9   10   11   12   13   14
acid   neutral   alkaline

Discoloration of the water results from disturbance of the peat layer (*left*). Composts must be washed well before use in aquaria (*right*).

Aquarium equipment

Composts

An aquarium compost is the gravel at the bottom of the tank in which plants can be grown. If a decorative tank is to be set up, the compost used is usually one of the gravels commercially available from a pet shop. These comprise a mixed gravel, usually fairly light in color and about $\frac{3}{16}$ inches in diameter. Coarser gravel makes rooting difficult and excess food and fish droppings tend to fall between the pieces and rot anaerobically (without CO_2) — usually becoming smelly and black. If the gravel is too fine all the residue rests on the top of the gravel. Plant growth can be encouraged by a layer of peat or soil under the compost. It should be used with care, however, for if a plant is uprooted, clouding of the water occurs. Planting sticks are useful for replanting (see page 142).

Lighting

Lighting displays fish to best advantage and helps plant growth. Most aquarists prefer to provide artificial lighting that they can regulate, rather than relying on daylight or ordinary room lighting. In any case, room lighting is useless for lighting an aquarium and a tank placed in strong sunlight will encourage algal growth, causing the water to turn green.

One 25-watt light bulb, either 'clear' or 'pearl', per square foot of water is usually sufficient, if left on for about ten hours a day. Fluorescent bulbs can be used in preference to ordinary light bulbs as these have a longer life. Bulbs emitting light at the red end of the spectrum give better plant growth than white light bulbs. Special bulbs for encouraging plant growth have been on the market in recent years.

Decorative lighting is popular with many aquarists. Underwater lighting, for instance, helps to heat the water as well as providing light.

(1) Low wattage light bulbs provide sufficient light for most tanks. (2) Direct sunlight causes algal blooms. (3) Fluorescent tubes can be used, and (4) units that provide heat as well as light.

Thermometers

As we have mentioned earlier, the temperature of aquarium water is very important, especially for tropical fishes. Too low a temperature makes fish sluggish and more susceptible to disease, but too high a temperature decreases the oxygen content of the water and the fish will rise to the surface, gasping for air. With experience, the aquarist can usually tell if a large change of temperature has occurred, but it is always advisable to have a thermometer available. Ideal temperatures should be achieved before introducing fish to the aquarium.

The most accurate type of thermometer uses mercury as the indicator and has the scale marked directly on the glass tube. These are difficult to obtain in the range required, however, and one usually has to settle for something less efficient. The most common type available has the glass tube mounted on a scaled, clear plastic strip, and it is held in position in the aquarium by a rubber sucker pad. Unfortunately, the coloring on the scale wears off, making it difficult to read.

Popular form of aquarium immersion heater available in varying wattages to suit tank size.

Alternative form of heating by an under gravel element.

A lamp which also serves to heat the water.

Heaters

To maintain the required temperature in a tropical aquarium some form of heating is necessary. To the aquarist with only one or two tanks, electricity is the most efficient method. Gas is far from odorless, and the control equipment would be too bulky. Usually, the electric heater consists of an element wound around an insulated core and contained in a heat-resisting glass tube. A rubber cork with the electric cable held tightly through it acts as a watertight seal. Another method of heating by electricity is to place tubular space heaters (normally rated at 60 watts per foot) beneath the tank so that the heat rises to heat the complete unit. This method can be usefully employed if a built-in unit has been constructed with adequate space between tanks, as the heat passing around the bottom tanks rises to help heat those on the upper layers. Care must be taken, however, to either mount the heater away from the glass bottom or to place a baffle between the tanks to avoid breaking the glass.

external thermostat

submersible thermostat

stick-on thermometer

Tank above is fitted with two types of thermostat and a thermometer, and that on the opposite page is fitted with three types of filter.

Thermostats

With the tropical aquarium it is necessary to control the temperature of the water within a range of 65-85° F, depending upon the species of fish concerned. Aquarium thermostats are operated by contraction and expansion of a bimetallic strip at the end of which there are electric contacts. To reduce arcing and electrical interference a small magnet near these contacts provides a snap action.

There are two general types of thermostat. First, there is the internal one which can be either fully or partly submerged in the water, the latter being clipped to the top frame of the tank, which means water levels cannot be allowed to fall very much. Second, the external thermostats are placed outside the tank fixed either by a metal clip or adhesive to the front glass. The manufacturer's instructions should be followed closely both in the wiring up and use of these thermostats. The temperature of any tank will always fluctuate a few degrees around the point set by the thermostat. This is a good thing, as slightly varying temperatures are better for the fish than a uniformly constant one. In their natural environment all tropical fish are subject to diurnal variations in water temperature.

Filters, although not essential, are helpful in keeping the water clear and freely circulating.

Air pumps

Air pumps are used in the aquarium for two purposes: to force air into the tank and to work filtration systems. Aeration consists of forcing air by means of the pump through a small porous stone (diffuser). The stream of small bubbles formed agitates the surface of the tank allowing better exchange of carbon dioxide and oxygen. In a properly kept tank, not overstocked with fish, there is usually no need for aeration.

In filtration systems the pump pushes water through a filter which is either inside or outside the tank. The filter contains a filtration medium of charcoal, peat, nylon wool, plastic foam, etc. and particles passing through the medium are filtered off, keeping the water clear and freely circulating. Another type is the under-gravel filter where the water is filtered through the aquarium compost. The common air pump is a small vibrator type which is very efficient but noisy. For the aquarist with more than four tanks, the electrical induction motor type of pump is more satisfactory. This is quiet in operation and drives one or two pistons, usually by a rotary movement, providing greater quantities of air. The cost of these very efficient pumps, however, is high.

25

Tank covers

Many species of tropical fish will jump from their normal element. It is essential, therefore, to have some form of cover over the top of the aquarium. We have already mentioned that some form of artificial lighting will be required so this cover can serve to hold the light bulbs and also help to prevent evaporation. Normally these covers are made from aluminum, a metal which is easily worked, does not corrode too readily and also reflects the light fairly well. However, in the special fiberglas tanks now produced, the hoods are made of the same material. When made with a small lip on the bottom edges to fit neatly into the tank top, any evaporation condenses on the cooler metal and runs back into the tank. At this point it must be emphasized that wiring connected to the bulb holders must be well maintained and replaced when the insulation becomes brittle. If this is not done, the risk of an electric shock is high. When tanks are placed in rows, an individual tank top is not required and sheets of glass form ideal covers. This glass can either be laid directly onto the tank top or special clips can be used.

Tank tops resting on a top metal frame tend to cause rusting.

Aquarium covers also keep out dust and reduce heat loss and evaporation. A cover may take the form of a plain glass sheet with clips (*left*) or a metal hood (*right*) housing light bulbs.

A tank cover is essential for lively fish like *Aphyosemion vexillifer.*

To prevent this a grooved rubber strip can be fixed around the frame edge or, alternatively, the top frame can be treated with a cold galvanizing preparation. For the latter process the existing paint and rust must be removed (for instance by rubbing down with the sander of an electric drill), all the loose particles wiped off and the preparation applied with a brush. When dry, two coats of paint are applied. This technique can be used on new and old frames and provides a very good protection from rust for many years.

A cold galvanizing process protects iron-frame tanks from rust. Modern stainless steel and frameless tanks are rust-free.

Contents of the aquarium

Snails

While snails are not an essential part of the healthy aquarium, as is commonly believed, they will certainly consume some of the food leftovers, some algae and plants and decayed vegetation. They will not touch fish excreta, however, and they increase the waste products in the tank by adding their own. There is also a danger that they will eat living plants if other forms of food are lacking. Snails are introduced into the aquarium on plants, either as eggs or as very tiny, newly hatched snails. Most reproduce by laying eggs in clusters contained in a jelly-like substance attached to firm objects such as rocks, glass or plants. When fresh plants are introduced to the aquarium it is nearly impossible to remove every egg without causing some damage to the plants. It is better to remove those which will come away easily and squash each tiny snail as it is noticed. If all are killed before maturity then the tank will remain free of snails.

An aquarium plant with egg clusters, showing damage by snails

Red Ramshorn (1), *Bullinus* (2) and Malayan snail (3)

One useful genus of snail, *Ampullaria,* however, is of use to the fish breeder in that the water in which it is kept breeds infusorians, minute organisms which form the food of newly hatched fish, at a very fast rate. The snails are kept in a tank on their own and fed on lettuce or cabbage leaves. Care must be taken not to overfeed or the resulting odor is not very pleasant.

The most common variety of snail seen in tropical aquaria is the Red Ramshorn *(Planorbis corneus).* Another snail in tropical aquaria, though not often seen because of its nocturnal habits, is the Malayan snail *(Melania tuberculata).* During the day, this snail spends its time burrowing into the gravel in search of food but at night it comes out, climbing all over the tank. This snail does not feed on growing plants preferring to feed on the bottom and is therefore helpful in removing decay from the tank. The Malayan snail is live-bearing and therefore does not spoil the appearance of the tank with unsightly masses of eggs.

Plants

Every aquarist should be able to grow healthy plants without too much effort. Sometimes the requirements of the fish and the plants clash. In the case of egg-laying toothcarps, which do not like bright light, it is not possible to grow plants in tanks set up specially for breeding these fish.

All plants have certain basic requirements. From the compost they get chemical salts such as calcium, phosphorus, nitrogen (as nitrates and nitrites) and very small quantities of other elements (trace elements). Fish also help to provide nitrogenous substances in their droppings. In a tank which has been set up and undisturbed for many years plant growth slows up; perhaps this is due to the exhaustion of the gravel. Changing old or adding new compost and gravel should replace the exhausted materials. Temperature is also important. Plants have a temperature at which they grow best, and this is probably higher than the optimum temperature (72°–75° F) for most fish.

Some aquarium plants grow best as bog plants with their roots in water and their leaves in the air, though the humidity has to be very high. Seeds of some aquatic plants

A popular aquarium plant,
Cryptocoryne beckettii

By photosynthesis, green plants manufacture sugars utilizing energy from the sun and carbon dioxide from the air.

must be germinated as bog plants in this way. Light is tremendously important for aquarium plants—its intensity, how long it is kept on, and quality of the light all affect growth. Plants reared in a greenhouse with polythene double-glazing, for instance, may be retarded in growth because of the altered wave length of light reaching them.

Other cryptocorynes grow well as bog plants.

water

compost

Plants of the genus *Vallisneria* are popular plants for aquaria. This genus originates mainly from tropical regions and is flower-producing.

1. *Vallisneria gigantea* is a large member of the genus with leaves up to 1 inch wide and 4 to 5 feet in length. It is more suitable for large, cold water aquaria as warm temperatures are not tolerated.

2. *Vallisneria spiralis* is the variety most commonly seen in tropical aquaria. The leaves normally grow up to 18 inches long and ½ inch wide. If given plenty of light, the leaves will lengthen and spread over the surface, but the runners will grow in profusion to provide the ideal background to the aquarium

3. *Vallisneria spiralis tortifolia* is another very well-known variety commonly called 'twisted vallis'. The leaves grow to about 12 inches but are much more brittle than the straight *Vallisneria* and can be easily broken if not treated with care.

4. *Vallisneria spiralis* 'contortionist' is a variety recently introduced to the aquarium. The leaves are much more twisted than *tortifolia* and are longer, spreading over the surface like normal *spiralis*.

Plants of the genus *Sagittaria* are similar in appearance to those of *Vallisneria*, but are suitable for nearly all sizes of aquaria. They are propagated mainly by runners and some species grow naturally in bog conditions, producing floating and aerial leaves.

5. *Sagittaria subulata* is the most common and popular plant of the genus. During spring and summer the leaves form narrow stems and spread into an oval, floating at the surface. This plant grows to a height of about 12 inches, but there is a smaller variety growing to about 8 inches.

6. *Sagittaria latifolia* is a large member of the genus and therefore suitable only for the largest aquaria. It produces broad strong leaves up to 24 inches long. Under favorable conditions this plant will produce aerial leaves and occasionally flowers. It is suitable for both cold and tropical aquaria.

7. *Bacopa* produces bright green rounded leaves in pairs on ascending stems. When the plant has grown too tall, it can be nipped off and replanted. *Bacopa caroliniana* is the best-known species.

8. There are three varieties of *Acorus* or 'Japanese Rush', two tall (one of which has yellow-and-green striped leaves) and one short. *Acorus* is a submerged bog plant which grows very slowly.

Without doubt, plants of the genus *Cryptocoryne* provide the aquarist with more color and variety than any other. About a dozen species are known to the aquarist, but there are about 40 in the genus, originating mainly from the Malay Archipelago. Species vary in size from small plants only 1 or 2 inches high, to large ones up to 2 feet high. Leaves range in color from pale green to deep red, and their shape ranges from slender and strap-like to broad and spade-like. However, the majority are really bog plants spending the rainy season totally submerged and gradually producing aerial leaves as the water evaporates. Because of this, many species are difficult to keep for any length of time, and those mentioned here will be hardy species generally obtainable.

Cryptocorynes have the advantage of growing very well in situations where the light is weak, but they are ornamental rather than useful plants. Their growth is slow and reproduction is by runners.

Nomenclature of the genus is often confused in the literature, but the following classification is the one most commonly accepted.

1. *Cryptocoryne affinis,* or *C. haerteliana,* is the most widely seen species with dark green upper surface and deep red underside to the leaves. Quite prolific, it grows to 12 inches. It thrives under subdued lighting.

2. *Cryptocoryne beckettii* is another fairly common variety. Its leaves have a soft, pale green upper surface and reddish-brown underside. It grows to 10 inches.

3. *Cryptocoryne griffithi* is a temperamental species which takes time to settle down. It prefers soft water. The leaves are green on top and brown underneath.

4. There are two varieties of *Cryptocoryne nevillii,* one short and one tall, both having the same basic characteristics. The leaves are bright green on both sides.

5. *Cryptocoryne willissii* is a species which varies considerably. It sometimes grows by extending the crown and producing a type of rhizome as the leaves die off. The leaves are green on top and brown underneath.

6. *Cryptocoryne ciliata* is a large species, growing up to 18 inches with pale green leaves. It grows best as a bog plant when the leaves become heart-shaped and much shorter.

35

The genus *Echinodorus* includes some of the largest plants seen in tropical aquaria, and all originated in the Americas. Quite a few are naturally bog plants, and if provided with plenty of light and space, they will produce aerial leaves and flowers. If pollinated, seeds will ripen and many small plants can be propagated. When aerial flowers are not produced, the flower stalk stays submerged and small plants develop at intervals along its length. All the species are green, varying from pale to dark, depending on the strength of light they receive. Leaf shape can be very variable, especially with species producing aerial leaves.

1. *Echindorus berteroi* (Cellophane plant) is a submerged plant, the older leaves of which are heart-shaped at the end of long stems. Aerial leaves and flowers are often produced.

2. Once established, the leaves of *Echinodorus cordifolius* remain the same shape whether aerial or submerged. When well fed, the leaves grow to 6 inches long and 4 inches wide and flower stalks are often produced in summer.

3. *Echinodorus martii* has long, strap-like leaves with wavy edges. Normally it does not produce aerial leaves and the flower stalk, if kept submerged, produces small plants.

4. *Echinodorus paniculatus* (Amazon Swordplant) is the best-known plant of this genus and has two distinct forms—one with narrow leaves and one with broad. The flower stalk normally stays submerged, producing new shoots.

5. The tiny *Echinodorus tenellus* (Pigmy Chain Swordplant) grows only 2 inches high and spreads by runners. It can easily become choked with blanket weed and care should be taken not to introduce the latter into the same tank.

6. *Echinodorus grisebachii* (Chain Swordplant) reproduces by runners along the surface of the compost and is easily cultivated. Careful handling of the delicate leaves is necessary.

7. *Echinodorus tunicatus* is a relatively recent introduction to aquarists. It has similar leaves to *E. cordifolius* but they are more pointed at the tip. The flower stalk tends to stay submerged and produces new shoots only.

Aponogeton species have a bulb or tuber from which roots and leaves develop. The plants go through a resting period during which the leaves die off but they reappear after a few months. Reproduction is from seeds produced on flower spikes above the water, although some species produce side shoots from the rhizome. Tropical distribution is restricted to Africa, Asia and Australia and a number are peculiar to the island of Madagascar.

1. *Aponogeton ulvaceus* is a beautiful aquarium plant with latticed, semi-translucent green leaves. However, the leaves are easily torn and the plant tends to regress in winter. Becomes large under favorable conditions.

2. The leaves of *Aponogeton undulatus* are also translucent but have wavy edges. This plant can grow to heights of 6 to 8 inches depending on the light intensity reaching the tank. Imported as small bulbs or tubers.

3. *Aponogeton crispus* has pale green translucent leaves with crinkled margins. This species is fond of strong light and its narrow stems will adapt themselves to the depth of water in the aquarium. Propagation is by division of the tuber.

4. *Aponogeton fenestralis* (Madagascar lace plant) is expensive and difficult to grow but is a truly magnificent aquarium plant. The skeleton-like leaves consist of a mere latticework of cross veins and do indeed resemble lace.

5. *Cabomba* is a plant that grows at a very fast rate and soon overcrowds the tank. Old stems should be cut back and new stems taken from the latest growth. There are two or three varieties with slightly varying leaves. This is one of the most beautiful aquarium plants but it is not suitable for beginners.

6. *Hygrophila polysperma* has pale green lanceolate leaves and if kept pruned will produce an attractive bush. It will become straggly if left, however. Propagated easily from rooted cuttings.

7. *Ludwigia natans* is a common aquarium plant, the leaves of which have a pale green surface with reddish-brown underneath. This plant has a tendency to grow up out of the water and really grows better as a bog plant.

8. *Myriophyllum* (water milfoil) is most suited to cold water but will survive in lower tropical temperatures. There are several species which resemble each other. Their fine, feathery foliage encourages spawning in breeding tanks.

9. *Nomaphila stricta* has large, bright green leaves. It is closely related to *Hygrophila* and also needs to be well pruned. It is a very attractive plant for most sizes of aquaria and grows well under most conditions.

1. *Azolla* is a very small green floating plant, sometimes known as 'fairy moss'. It forms a dense covering which varies in color from brilliant green to a dark red in strong light. There are two or three varieties known to aquarists, all having the same characteristics.

2. There are two species of *Ceratopteris*—*C. cornuta* and *C. thalictroids*—known respectively as 'Floating' and 'Indian' Fern. Both plants reproduce by the formation of small plants on the edge of the leaves. In good light this is a very prolific plant.

3. *Lemna* is the duckweed to be seen floating on most ponds. It normally has small, round leaves, but one species, *L. trisulca*, has leaves shaped like ivy leaves. Some tropical fish eat this weed, and it is a good producer of shade in a tank where there is too much top light.

4. *Eichornia crassipes* (water hyacinth) has swollen leaf stems forming small buoyancy tanks to support the plant. This is a particularly showy plant for the large

aquarium, but needs strong daylight for good growth and therefore tends to die during winter. It produces an attractive, short-lived purple flower. Inset (4a) shows plant profile.

5. Commonly known as water lettuce, *Pistia* has thick fleshy leaves and resembles a floating lettuce. In good daylight, runners are produced in profusion and the long thick roots offer perfect cover for young fry. This plant thrives in tanks without covers, exposed to daylight.

6. *Riccia*, sometimes known as crystalwort, forms a floating mat just below the water surface. It sometimes becomes very thick, however, and needs to be thinned periodically. The pale green

leaves offer perfect refuge for fry and, in fact, the plant is popular among breeders of live-bearers. This plant is common in Australian waters.

7. The oval-shaped leaves of *Salvinia* are produced in pairs along the floating stems. It multiplies rapidly in strong light and quickly covers the aquarium surface. According to some authorities this plant has no roots— what appear to be roots are finely divided leaves.

8. *Najas* is a brittle, floating plant which also grows well if anchored to the gravel. It needs regular pruning to prevent it from becoming too straggly. There are two or three species of this plant.

Jawless fishes

Placoderms

Cartilaginous fishes

Bony fishes

Ostracoderms

Reptiles

Lungfishes

Amphibians

Lobe fins

Labyrinthodonts

Mammals

crocodiles

Coelacanths

marsupials

birds

monotremes

placentals

turtles

pterosaurs

lizards

dinosaurs

42

THE FISH

Evolution of the fish

The evolution of fish and modern animals is difficult to trace because the fossil record is incomplete. However, enough is known to suggest the general pattern of evolution and to reconstruct in some detail the history of groups in those areas where fossils abundantly occur. The chart on the opposite page shows relationships among the major groups of vertebrates; those animals within a given color probably developed from common ancestors.

Fossil evidence has demonstrated that the birds and mammals arose from cold-blooded reptiles, the reptiles from the amphibians, the amphibians from some of the primitive fish and the fish themselves from even more primitive vertebrates that were probably derived from invertebrate stock. The evidence also shows that the incredible number of diverse fish forms that exists today is but a fraction of the total number of fish that have existed in the past, either in marine or freshwater environments. The existing forms have obviously been the most successful in the struggle for existence and may be considered, for the time being anyway, the topmost twigs of the fish family tree. The less successful forms, known to us through fossils, can be thought of as the lower branches, some of which are short, others longer and themselves branched. These will represent the earlier forms that perhaps flourished for a time but eventually failed to adapt to a change in their environment and so perished and became extinct.

The evolution of the early vertebrate larval forms to primitive fish-like forms is unrecorded in the fossil history of fish, probably because both forms were soft-bodied animals. By the time fish-like fossils were discovered, the jawless fish, the cartilaginous fish and the bony fish were already differentiated from each other and are represented by a number of diverse and often specialized types.

Of these, the bony fish have been the most successful and today are the most abundant, diverse and complex group of fish. It has been estimated that 20,000 species exist, they have adapted themselves to widely varying conditions in sea water, brackish estuarine environments and fresh water.

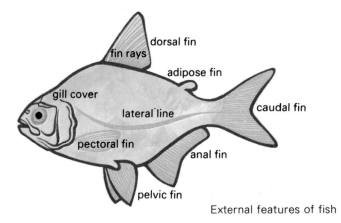

External features of fish

Physical structure of fish

There are many modifications of the general external features shown above. The egg-laying tooth-carps (see page 64) have a larger anal fin and large pectoral fins and some fish, for example the Australian rainbowfish *(Melanotaenia nigrans)* (see page 114), have two dorsal fins. In the angelfish the pelvic fins are considerably modified (see page 110).

Fin rays are divided into hard rays (those with spines) and soft rays. The form and number of fin rays are characteristic of the species and expressed as a fin formula (e.g., D = dorsal fin); roman numerals indicate true hard rays, arabic numerals, soft rays. Thus, the dorsal fin formula of the fire-mouth cichlid *(Cichlasoma meeki)* is D.XV–XVI/9–10. Longitudinal and transverse scale counts are also characteristic of species and

Scales in black are used in longitudinal and transverse scale counts

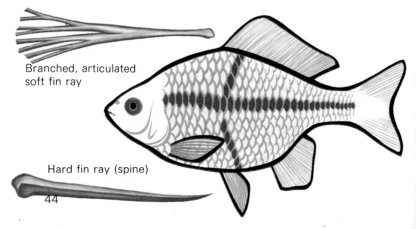

Branched, articulated soft fin ray

Hard fin ray (spine)

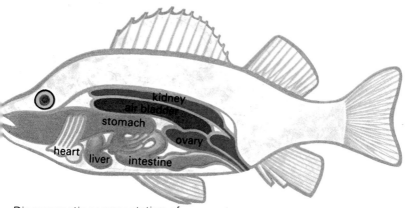

Diagrammatic representation of internal organs of fish.

used in systematic identification.

The internal organs of bony fish are much alike in general appearance. The function of the air bladder is not completely known but in several families, collectively called the Ostariophysi, it is connected with the auditory apparatus. The reproductive organs are paired and closely connected with the excretory system. Eggs are discharged from the ovary down the oviduct to the urogenital sinus and the exterior. The sperm is discharged from the testis, down the vas deferens which runs alongside the kidney and into the seminal vesicle which connects with the urogenital sinus. The skin consists of two layers, a thin epidermal layer and a thicker dermal layer which produces the scales and also the mucus which covers the body.

Humpy-back is a skeletal deformity that occasionally occurs in fish.

Classification

Fish, like most living creatures, have two names, a popular name and a scientific, or Latin, name. Popular names are easy to pronounce and are vaguely descriptive but can lead to a great deal of confusion. For example, a Tiger Barb may be *Capoeta tetrazona, Capoeta partipentazona* or *Barbodes hexazona,* depending upon which part of the world you live in. The scientific names, on the other hand, are fixed by international scientific agreement and are worldwide in application. This method consists of giving a fish a 'surname' (name of the genus to which it belongs) and a special name (species name) which is specific to that fish. For example, the popular swordtail belongs to the genus *Xiphophorus* and is species *helleri.* The close relationship with the platy is easily seen as the platy is *Xiphophorus maculatus.* The specific name will sometimes describe a characteristic of the fish (e. g., *trilineata,* three-lined) or may describe its origin (*senegalensis,* Senegal) or be named after its collector or describer. Occasionally a sub-species may exist and a third name is then added.

Fish belong to the phylum Chordata, that is, animals with backbones. The superclass Pisces includes four classes of fish. The Placoderms are now extinct. The Agnatha, or jaw-less fish, have only a few living members. Sharks and rays, with cartilaginous skeletons, belong to the class Chondrichthyes. All the fish considered here are bony fish and members of the class Osteichthyses.

Common names often lead to confusion. *Gambusia afinis afinis* (1). *Gambusia afinis holbooki* (2) and *Heterandria formosa* (3) are all known as Mosquito fish

46

The animal kingdom can be represented as a tree on which the main branches represent *phyla,* and smaller branches *classes*

These classes are further divided into orders and families and then into genera and species. It is of importance to the aquarist to know generally into which family a fish fits as genera in the same family tend to have similar habitats and breeding patterns. In this section of the book, species from those families most popular among tropical freshwater aquarists are described and illustrated. The arrangement may differ from others, but classifications often vary from authority to authority.

SUPERCLASS
Pisces

CLASS Agnatha
Jawless Fish – Lampreys

CLASS Placodermi
all extinct

ORDER Isospondyli

ORDER Ostariophysi

SUB-ORDER
Cyprinoidei

SUB-ORDE
Siluroidei

FAMILY Mormyridae

FAMILY Cyprinidae

FAMILY Characidae

FAMILY Callichthyidae

FAMILY Pantodontidae

FAMILY Lorica

Pantodon buchholzi

Hyphessobrycon innesi

Corydoras melanistius

Mormyrops boulengeri

Serrasalmus rhombeus

Plecostomus pu

Copeina arnoldi

Carassius auratus
auratus

Barbus filamentosus

Brachydanio rerio

48

CLASS Chondrichthyes
Sharks, Rays

CLASS Osteichthyes
Bony Fish

ORDER Microcyprini

ORDER Percomorphi

FAMILY Poecilidae

FAMILY
Monodactyloidae

FAMILY Anabantidae

FAMILY
Cyprinodontidae

FAMILY Cichlidae

Live-bearing
tooth-carps

Egg-laying
tooth-carps

Lebistes reticulatus

Scatophagus argus

Betta splendens

Mollienesia sphenops

Trichopsis vittatus

Aphyosemion australe

Cichlastoma meeki

Symphosodon discus

Distribution of the live-bearing tooth-carps

Family Poeciliidae (live-bearing tooth-carps)

From the map it can be seen that the live-bearing tooth-carps are restricted in nature to two parts of the world, and the majority comes from the Americas. Known technically as *ovoviviparous* fish, they do not reproduce in the same way as mammals. That is to say, once the female has produced the egg, no further direct attachment to the mother takes place. The eggs are held within the female in a brood pouch and are fertilized there by the male. The eggs develop and later hatch, but the young are not released until they have completely developed. By then, they are miniatures of their parents and within minutes of birth are capable of eating and swimming normally.

Nature has provided the male live-bearers with a special means of fertilizing the females. At puberty, the anal fin of the male undergoes a complete change and bears no resemblance to that of the female. After the change, the fin is called a *gonopodium* and is then used exclusively for the injection of sperm into the female.

Normally the gonopodium points backward, but when mating takes place it is twisted forward and sideways and the tip is inserted in the female's vent. At this moment, the male ejects his sperm which travels along a groove in the gonopodium and enters the female to fertilize the eggs.

It takes about one month for the young to develop, but this period can be varied by high or low temperatures. However,

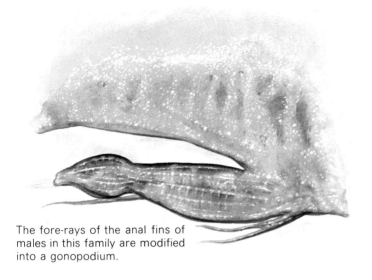

The fore-rays of the anal fins of males in this family are modified into a gonopodium.

it does not follow that by increasing the water temperature the period of gestation will be shortened. The numbers produced in each brood can also vary quite appreciably; young females produce up to 50 offspring, but the more mature they become the greater the numbers — up to 200 on occasion. Each female can produce four or five broods from the single initial fertilization.

The professional breeder who wishes to maintain a good strain will remove all the males from the growing brood as soon as they are recognized. This prevents the females from being indiscriminately fertilized. Later, the most suitable partnerships can be induced for the production of superior offspring.

It has been known for some time that some members of this family have been able to change their sex. This reversal seems to be encouraged by high temperature and usually occurs in spring and summer. The most quoted example is that of female swordtails developing a 'sword' and gonopodium before bearing young. These fish have been used scientifically by the late Dr. Myron Gordon of New York in genetic studies and Dr. Alex Comfort of London in his research into the aging processes.

In the Poeciliidae, over 40 species and sub-species are available to the aquarist, and many color varieties have been developed by cross and line breeding. If well fed and looked after they will live to five years of age, according to size.

Breeding live-bearers

Breeding live-bearers is not difficult. In fact, if there is a male and a female of the same species in a tank it is almost certain that they are breeding. The males are persistent in their courtship, giving the females little peace, and within a few hours of placing them together the female will be fertilized. It is better to have two, if not more, females to each male to allow a little respite.

Most fish, especially if not well fed on live foods, will eat their tiny offspring if given the opportunity and live-bearers are no exception. It is therefore imperative that some means of protecting the brood from their cannibalistic parents is provided. In the wild, as soon as they are born, the young instinctively head for the nearest cover. In the aquarium, if adequate cover is provided in the form of plants of various kinds most of the fry will survive. The ideal floating plants are *Riccia* and Indian fern, and plants such as *Myriophyllum* afford cover at the bottom of the aquarium. This method is somewhat haphazard as not accurate count can be made and trapping needs to be adopted if all the brood is to be saved. Infusoria (minute organisms) are not necessary as food except for fry of the smaller species, and a few hours after birth fry of most species will eat dust-fine dried food. Food should be offered at least three or four times a day. The lengthening of the anal fin in the first few weeks distinguishes the males from the females.

Female live-bearer releasing young. The number of young delivered varies with the species and with the age of the female.

Examples of easily constructed
breeding traps for live-bearers

When only one female is involved in breeding, a commercially produced breeding trap can be used. This isolates the ex-
pectant mother in a small cage suspended within an aquarium.
The fry, when born, escape to the main tank through narrow
gaps in the bottom of the trap. Care must be exercised when
transferring the female to the trap. If more than one female is
to be used, a much larger trap is required and the aquarist will
have to make his own. With this method, all males and females
should live permanently in the trap. A large plexiglass box
with glass rods in the base can be assembled, but a much easier
way is to use a plastic mesh. This is sold by most garden shops
for horticultural uses. By cutting, bending and joining, large
rigid 'nets' can be made and suspended in a large tank, and the
fry are then able to escape in all directions. If large enough, up
to a dozen pairs of adults can be accommodated in this way
and virtually a continuous supply of offspring provided.
Alternatively, a large trap can be assembled from V-shaped
sheets of glass arranged as shown above.

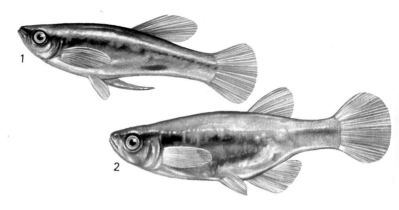

Examples of wild types of guppies (1, 2) from which the other more elaborate varieties shown have been bred. The Green Lace Guppy (3) for example, has a beautiful lace pattern on the body and the Scarf-tail Guppy (4) has a tail often much longer than the body of the fish.

The guppy (Lebistes reticulatus)

Because of its low cost and hardiness this is the most common of all tropical fish seen in aquaria. Many people start off with a few plain guppies before purchasing other more expensive types, and in spite of some common errors often made at first they usually survive, eventually to breed.

A native of some of the islands of the Caribbean and the bordering countries of South America, the wild guppy is quite plain in comparison with its aquarium-bred relatives. From these insignificant fish have come the most beautiful and varied hybrids, and many aquarists have given up all other

Because of its magnificent tail the Veil-tail Guppy (5) is possibly the most popular of all hybrids available at present. The female Golden Double Sword Guppy (6) exhibits an attractive golden color. Other guppy strains can be distinguished by their dorsal and tail fins (7).

fish to specialize solely in guppies, becoming internationally well known for their special strains. Until recently, the females have changed very little, but now, by selective breeding, color is appearing in the tail. The males have shown amazing development, and the illustrations above show some of the strains that have become 'fixed'.

The mixed strain from a dealer's stock tank can be bought quite cheaply, but if the aquarist wishes to purchase a new or special strain, he must expect to pay a considerably higher price for the time and patience of the breeder.

Black or Midnight Molly
(*Mollienesia* sp.)

Mollies (*Mollienesia sp*)

Although popular live-bearers, members of this particular genus are not so easy to keep as those of the genera *Lebistes* and *Xiphophorus*. All the members of the genus come from South and Central America. The water in which they live is hard and alkaline and the normal temperature is around 80° F, higher than that recommended for the community tank. This combination produces an appreciable growth of algae, which forms a large part of the diet of these fish.

To maintain these fish in good condition, these requirements need to be met in the aquarium and it is therefore advisable to provide them with a special tank to themselves. As these fish frequent brackish water in nature, a small quantity of salt, about one teaspoonful to the gallon, can be added to the aquarium. The mouth of the molly is turned upward so they are well equipped to take dried food, and if fairly strong lighting is used algae will be provided naturally. Dried foods with a vegetable content should be used if possible.

It is possible to breed these fish in outdoor ponds during the summer months, for they will tolerate a temperature range of 60°–90° F.

Mollienesia sphenops is the short-finned member of the genus. These fish are widespread in their natural distribution.

It is somewhat more hardy than *latipinna* and it can be used in the community aquarium with some care. Unfortunately, because of continual line breeding, the average length attained by this fish is only about 2 inches, although really good fish will reach 3½ inches. These are usually bred by the enthusiast by introducing new fish regularly into his strain. The species varies considerably in coloration, but in general the coloring of the female is more uniform than that of the male.

The Sail-fin Molly *(Mollienesia latipinna)* is by far the more attractive molly, but it is more demanding in its requirements. The male of the species develops a very large sail-like dorsal fin that can reach to an inch above the fish. The normal form has a metallic blue background color with dots of yellow, red and green. By crossing with the Black Molly and then line breeding the progeny, a molly with a black sail fin has been produced— a magnificent fish, but very rare.

Another species, the Giant Sail-fin Molly *(Mollienesia velifera),* is similar to the Sail-fin Molly except that, as the name suggests, it grows slightly larger, often to a length of 5 to 6 inches under good conditions. Aquarium specimens rarely reach a length of more than 4 inches, however.

Giant Sail-fin Molly
(*Mollienesia velifera*)

Swordtails and platies (Xiphophorus sp)
The swordtail *(Xiphophorus helleri)* is another fish which, by selective breeding, has produced a wide variety of colors but has not changed the basic body and fin shape. However, the native fish of this species, known as the Green Swordtail, is very attractive and can still be seen in many tanks. Unfortunately, by continuously breeding from the same strains the fish have been reduced in size, and it is a rare specimen that reaches the 5-inch growth of the wild fish. Distributed from Southern Mexico to Guatemala, the wild males and females are approximately the same size if the male's sword is disregarded. Males are slimmer in outline than females.

Very often this fish is selected by the beginner because of its attractive color, but it is not always a wise choice. Because swordtails grow fairly large, the other members of the tank tend to move away when one approaches. Very often the males chase the other fish and also appropriate much of the available food, aggravating the situation by their increasing size. It is advisable, therefore, to allow the smaller members of the aquarium to settle down and grow before introducing swordtails.

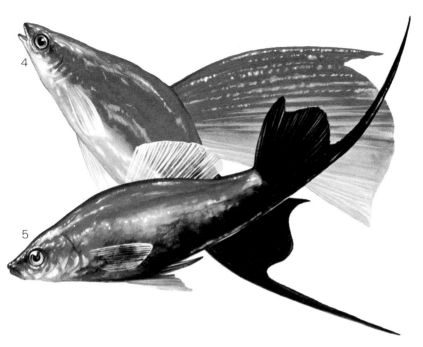

The normal variety Green Swordtail (1) is still popular with many aquarists. The Red-eyed Swordtail (2), as its name suggests, has red eyes. The Red Wagtail Swordtail (3) displays jet-black finnage. It is an attractive fish and very popular among aquarists. 'Simpson' Swordtail (4) is a mutation from America, named after its breeder. By further interbreeding the flowing dorsal fin has been passed on to all the known types. The patterns on the Berlin Swordtail (5) look haphazard but in fact the general outlines have been fixed. By further line breeding an all-black fish has been produced.

To obtain the best results when keeping swordtails, large tanks should be used to allow space for the fish to move and grow. As with the mollies, some algae should be included in their diet, although with swordtails this is not quite as important. It must be remembered that if more than one type of swordtail, or for that matter two different members of this genus, are in the same aquarium, cross breeding will take place. If the types are to remain pure, than a separate aquarium for each is essential.

The related platy *(Xiphophorus maculatus)* is shorter, has a more solid appearance and, most important, has no aggressive tendencies. The males, except for the gonopodium, are like the females but slightly smaller and slimmer and do not develop the typical sword of the swordtail. The platy was once mistakenly thought to be a member of the genus *Platypoecilus* from which the popular name was derived. Many hybrids have been produced.

The platy is a hardy fish, makes few demands and is undoubtedly a most suitable live-bearer for the beginner. With a little experience and one or two spare tanks the aquarist can try his hand at producing his own hybrids. As with other live-bearers, platies prefer hard, alkaline water with a temperature between 75°–80° F. If the aquarium is well lit, sufficient algae for their needs will develop naturally.

Another species of this genus often seen is the Variegated Platy *(Xiphophorus variatus)*. Hybridization has taken place

The sequence of crosses involved in producing the platy variety Golden Wagtail. The first cross is between a gold and a wild gray platy.

first cross

second cross

third cross

60

female

male

male

Two male Variegated Platies (*Xiphophorus variatus*) chasing a female, with the variety Red Platy (*top left*).

and also cross breeding between this and other members of the genus. The main characteristic is that the male and the female do not always have the same color patterns. The female generally has an overall golden color with very little of the color contrasts displayed by the male.

The platies are much more reliable breeders. They can be left with their young with reasonable safety, provided the parents are well fed and the tank is well planted.

Other live-bearers

The Pike Top Minnow or Pike Live-bearer *(Belonesox belizanus)* must be given its own tank and fed only on live foods, preferably small fish. When adult at 6 to 8 inches it can eat most small fish in a tropical aquarium, and is, in fact, the largest species of live-bearer.

Pike Top Minnow (1); Mosquito Fish (2); Dwarf Top Minnow (3);
One-sided Live-bearer (4)

The Mosquito Fish *(Gambusia affinis),* although small, is
not very popular because of its tendency of fin-nipping. It is
used extensively in natural mosquito control in the tropics as
each fish can destroy its own weight in mosquito larvae every
day. It is usually gray in color, but in a sub-species *G. holbrooki,*
the males are nearly all black.

The Dwarf Top Minnow *(Heterandria formosa)* is the
smallest of the live-bearers, the males reaching a maximum of
only one inch, the females a little larger. They are best kept in a
tank of their own when they will multiply rapidly if well fed.

The One-sided Live-bearer *(Jenynsia lineata)* is not often
seen in the aquarium because the older males tend to be aggressive. The males are very interesting scientifically because of
restricted movement in the gonopodium, a modified fin that
serves for the introduction of sperm — in some it is movable to
the left, in others to the right. 'Right-handed' males can only
mate with 'left-handed' females and vice versa.

The Hump-back Limia *(Limia nigrofasciata)* is the most attractive member of its genus. The males develop the hump at maturity. Broods are small in number, with a longer gestation period than usual. A trap is necessary for breeding as the females tend to eat the young. The dorsal fin in the male becomes enlarged and fan-like with age.

The Blindfish *(Amblyopsis spelaeus)* has its origin in the southern United States. This very interesting fish has many sensory vibratory receptors on the head and body.

The Half-beak *(Dermgenys pusillus)* is one of the few live-bearers from the 'old world'. It is not easy to keep as it requires such foods as *Daphnia* and mosquito larvae. A small quantity of salt in the aquarium is beneficial for breeding and a trap is necessary. The fish tend to float just below the surface.

Anableps anableps is rarely seen in the aquarium but is of interest in that its eyes are mounted in elevated sockets enabling it to see above the surface. The sexes are 'right-and left-handed' and only opposites can mate as in *Jenynsia*.

Hump-back Limia (5); Blindfish (6); Half-beak (7); *Anableps* (8)

Distribution of the egg-laying tooth-carps

Family Cyprinodontidae (egg-laying tooth-carps)

Members of this family are closely related to the live-bearing tooth-carps. They are small fish with interesting breeding habits and have relatively large mouths well filled with teeth, thereby enabling them to eat other species smaller than themselves. They need soft, acid water and temperatures between 68°–73° F; they prefer live food and dislike bright light. They are excellent jumpers, so tanks must have tightly fitting lids. For breeding purposes they can be classified as *egg-hangers*, which lay their eggs on the roots of floating plants, or *egg-buriers*, which bury their eggs in mud at the bottom of ponds.

Examples from the two groups of egg-layers

Egg hangers
Asphanius
Panchax
Oryzias
most *Aphyosemion* sp
Chriopeops goodei
Jordanella florididae
Fundulus
Rivulus
Cubanichthys cubensis
Valencia hispanica
Aplocheilus
Aplocheilichthys
Micropanchax
Epiplatys
Pachypanchax

Egg buriers
Roloffia occidentalis
Aphyosemion sjoestedti
Cynolebias
Rachovia brevis
Cynopoecilus
Pterolebias
Nothobranchius

Breeding egg-hangers

To breed these fish, very soft water (under 50 ppm $CaCO_3$) is necessary, and rain water or a mixture of demineralized water and tap water can be used. The next operation is to dissolve four handfuls of natural peat in rain water, bring it to a boil, allow it to cool, and squeeze it dry. This peat should be added to the rain water in the breeding tank, where it will settle on the bottom in a few days. The boiling treatment adjusts the pH of the peat to between 5.5 and 6.5.

A breeding mop for the tank can be made from a cork and nylon wool and is much more suitable than floating plants as it can be sterilized. The mop should be situated in the darkest corner of the tank for the fish do not favor light.

When preparations for breeding are complete, one healthy male should be placed with three females in the tank. Very soon he will drive the females around, then eggs will be laid, two or three at a time, perhaps on several occasions each day, onto the mop. In one week as many as 250 eggs may be laid. The male is so virile that if he is given only one female he will kill her.

At the end of the week the mop can be removed to a jar filled with water from the tank and the eggs incubated at 68°–73° F. If a new mop is put in the tank, the adults will continue to spawn. The eggs will take 14 to 24 days to hatch, but developing embryos are easily seen at the end of one week. If the mop is not removed from the tank after one week, well-developed fish may eat the newly hatched fry.

Breeding tank with peat layer suitable for egg-hangers

breeding mop

soft acid water at 68-73°F

A selection of egg-hangers available to the aquarist
Rivulus cylindraceus comes from Cuba and Florida and grows to about 2½ inches in length. It is a good leaper and needs a close fitting cover on the tank. It is said to leave the water to rest on top of floating leaves.

Aplocheilus lineatus grows to 4 inches in length. It has a large mouth and tends to eat any fish smaller than itself. One male needs more than one female when spawning. It lives in the wild in drainage ditches, pools, ponds and streams.

The Firemouth Panchax *(Epiplatys chaperi)* comes from West Africa. It swims just under the water surface waiting for food. A typical egg-hanger, it is fairly robust and lives well in the community tank. It can be a prolific spawner.

Pachypanchax playfairi originates from East Africa and is a large and tough member of the family. Its large mouth renders it unsuitable for the community tank. Like all the egg-laying tooth-carps, it is a valuable fish in the wild for malaria control as it consumes large amounts of mosquito larvae.

Aphyosemion australe australe is a very beautiful member of this genus which does well if given the correct conditions. It originated in West Africa. Females of species in this family are drab compared with the males and tend to resemble each other. To avoid confusion, therefore, it is important not to mix females if more than one species are kept.

Aphyosemion calliurum calliurum has become a very popular fish in recent years and is very easy to breed if given the right conditions. The colors in the dorsal and caudal fins are particularly variable. This fish forms hybrids with other aphyosemions.

Aphyosemion bivittatum bivittatum is a very pretty fish and spawns in the same way as other egg-hangers. This fish is slow to mature and is six months old before breeding begins.

Aphyosemion christyi may lay as many as 50 very sticky eggs all over the mop in a day. In an extensive study of these fish, it was found that 30 percent of all eggs laid were infertile and that the fertile eggs hatched in 15 days at 72° F.

Rivulus cylindraceus (1); *Aplocheilus lineatus* (2); Firemouth Panchax (3); *Pachypanchax playfairi* (4); *Aphyosemion australe australe* (5); *A. calliurum* (6); *A. bivittatum bivittatum* (7); *A. christyi* (8)

67

dry season

developing eggs survive in mud

adult fish dies as pond dries up

young hatch within a few hours of rain and rapidly mature

after spawning, mature fish buries eggs in mud

wet season

Diagrammatic life cycle of the egg-buriers

Egg-buriers
These fish have a fascinating life cycle in the wild as the parents die of asphyxia when ponds dry up during the dry season. The Dwarf Argentine Pearlfish *(Cynolebias nigripinnis)* provides an excellent example of the breeding habits of the egg-buriers.

The tank should be set up as for egg-hangers but without the mop. One male is usually placed with three females. If two adult males are placed with females very fierce fighting takes place. The male will court the females, dashing from one to the other, and eventually one of the females will begin to spawn. The male and female will dive together into the peat

Blue Gularis
(*Aphyosemion sjoestedti*)

Nothobranchius palmquisti

Dwarf Argentine Pearlfish
(*Cynolebias nigripinnis*)

Golden Pheasant
(*Roloffia occidentalis*)

Example of egg-buriers available to the aquarist

and completely disappear. After about 20 seconds the male will emerge, followed 10 seconds later by the female; an egg is left buried in the peat. The spawning process is repeated, but after 10 days the females become thin and are best removed and reconditioned for a week before being put back with the male.

The peat should be filtered through a nylon net which holds back the mold containing the eggs. It is advisable to put this in a plastic box and to leave it for a few days, until it has become moderately dry. A lid should be put on the box, which is then incubated at 68°–70° F for 16 weeks. Then, if soft acid water is added, the fry hatch within 12 hours.

Tiger Barb

Minnow

Family Cyprinidae (carp or carp-like fish)

The carp or carp-like fish consist of about 1,500 species some of which are important food fish. Many are small but some of the larger barbs, *Barbus tor,* for example, can grow up to 100 inches in length. Goldfish, many tropical species and well-known coarse fish, such as Roach, Tench and carp, belong to this family.

The Minnow *(Phoxinus phoxinus)* is a cold-water European cyprinid and one of the popular 'tiddlers' caught by small boys. Aquaria for minnows should have a gravel bottom, fresh water and aeration. Minnows eat all live foods, and a shoal will spawn on the bottom in water less than 6 inches deep.

The Goldfish *(Carassius auratus)* is the domesticated variety of the Asian sub-species known in China for 1,000 years. Goldfish eat both vegetable and animal foods and will spawn in large tanks and ponds. The grotesque shapes produced in

Comet Goldfish

Goldfish

Fantail Goldfish

Shubunkin

goldfish have been exploited by the Chinese and Japanese, and line breeding has given rise to various fancy varieties. The Comet, for example, is very similar to the typical cultivated form of the goldfish except for its very long caudal fin. The fantail has greatly elongated fins and is golden in color. Throwbacks to the wild type sometimes occur in spawning. The Telescope Fantail is similar but has protruding eyes. The Shubunkin is a very common variegated form of the goldfish, with colors of deep blue, red and white, black and gold. First-class specimens are expensive and the standards for showing internationally determined. The Eggfish has a stocky egg-shaped body with fins only moderately developed. There is no dorsal fin and the caudal fin is short and often double. The Celestial has a similar body form but has prominent globular eyes, directed upward. The Lionhead is an Eggfish in which the head is expanded with warty outgrowths.

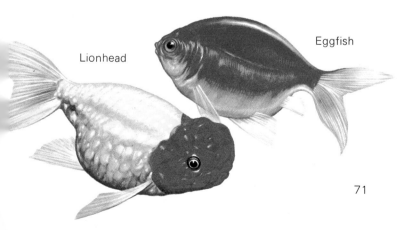

Lionhead

Eggfish

Danios

The Zebra Danio *(Brachydanio rerio)* is probably the most popular of the egg-laying tropicals. Because it is hardy and easy to breed, its cost is always low. It is an active fish and likes to have plenty of room in which to swim, as do all the danios.

The Pearl Danio *(B. albolineatus)* and the Spotted Danio *(B. nigrofasciatus)* are similar in shape to the Zebra Danio. The former has a silver body with an iridescent, mother-of-pearl effect giving differing colors depending on the angle of reflected light. The latter has stripes down the lateral line and numerous spots below. Their size is also similar, reaching 2 to 2½ inches in length. A more recent introduction is the Leopard Danio *(B. frankei)* which has a body pattern very much like trout. The Giant Danio *(Danio malabaricus)* grows to 4 inches in length and, although large, is a peaceful fish.

Breeding all species can be accomplished easily by placing a pair of fish in shallow water with a layer of previously sterilized pebbles or marbles in the bottom.

Zebra Danio (1); Pearl Danio (2); Spotted Danio (3); Giant Danio (4)

White Cloud Mountain Minnows

Found in the streams of the White Cloud Mountain in China, there are two distinct fish grouped under the same common name. The fish usually seen is *Tanichthys albonubes;* the other is *Aphyocypris pooni.* The only difference in appearance between them is a yellow edging to the fins of the latter.

These are peaceful little fish, ideal for the beginner as they are undemanding in their requirements. These fish are not true tropicals in nature and therefore high temperatures are not appreciated, 70°–75° F being most suitable. Spawning is easy. If two or three pairs are placed in a well-planted tank they will spawn and the fry will not be eaten if the parents are well fed. The young are even more attractive than the adult fish. The lateral line develops into a brilliant green stripe when the fry are about ⅓-inch long, far outshining the Neon Tetra at this stage. Unfortunately, as the fish grows, this line of color loses much of its brilliance and fades into a creamy stripe, but the fins turn to yellow and red.

Aphyocypris pooni (5); *Tanichthys albonubes* (6); fry (7)

Eyespot Rasbora

Rasbora leptosoma

Harlequin Fish

Spotted Rasbora

A selection of rasboras suitable for inclusion in the community aquarium. Most are shoaling species and probably 'community breeders'.

Rasboras

All natives of southeast Asia, members of the genus *Rasbora* are difficult to breed and, as a result, most fish are imported from that area, mainly from Singapore. The Harlequin Fish (*Rasbora heteromorpha*) is so common in the wild that it can be caught and flown to Western markets to sell at a price cheaper than if it had been bred artificially. This species is, however, the only one regularly seen; others are shipped in every now and then but their prices are usually high. All species prefer soft, acid water at temperatures between 75°–80° F and a well-planted aquarium providing areas of light and shade. They are peaceful fish and, if possible, should be purchased in a group as they like to school. They eat nearly anything, but prefer live foods such as *Daphnia* and micro-worms.

The Spotted or Pygmy Rasbora *(Rasbora maculata)* measures only one inch in length at maturity, whereas the Scissorstail *(Rasbora trilineata)* grows to 4 inches.

Barbs

Until a few years ago, most of the barbs were classified in the genus *Barbus,* but recent studies have split them into genera *Barbodes, Capoeta* and *Puntius.*

Most barbs are active, even boisterous and do not like overcrowding, preferring a well-aerated, well-planted tank. The majority have large scales producing changes in pattern under differing lighting conditions. They all breed readily in the aquarium.

Most common is the Tiger Barb *(Capoeta tetrazona)*, one of the most colorful and active of the barbs. It has an unfortunate tendency to nip the fins of other fish, but this is not so important when other barbs are involved. Males are distinguishable by their red 'snouts' and brighter colors. Some varieties of barbs are described on the next two pages.

A pair of Tiger Barbs showing sex differences

female

male

75

Barbodes hexona, although a very pretty barb, is not often seen as it is difficult to breed and does not travel well. It grows to 2½ inches, is quiet and spends most of its time among the plants.

The Tinfoil Barb *(Barbodes schwanenfeldi)* is a really beautiful fish but outside the scope of the average aquarist as it grows to at least 8 inches. It needs a predominantly vegetable diet or it will begin to eat the aquarium plants.

The Checkered Barb *(Capoeta oligolepis)* is easy to keep and breed and because of its size it does well in small tanks. It is a very attractive fish and grows to 2 inches in length. The males are most colorful at breeding time.

Females of the Half-banded Barb *(Capoeta semifasciolatus)* grow larger than the males, reaching 3 inches in length. The males have an intermittent black line along their sides, but the females have only an odd dot. The Golden Barb variety is probably related to *Puntius sachsi.* This is a fish without any striking beauty and yet is very popular with many aquarists.

Barbodes hexona (1); Tinfoil Barb (2); Checkered Barb (3); Half-banded Barb (4)

The males of the Cherry Barb *(Capoeta titteya)* develop a deep red color when spawning which is not as intense at other times. When breeding this species, shallow water and plenty of plants help prevent the parents from eating the eggs. This is a quiet fish, growing to about 2 inches, and ideal for the beginner.

The male Rosy Barb *(Puntius conchonius)* also exhibits brilliant mating colors. With black fins and a deep red body turning to green on the back he puts his mate to shame. Her colors are similar but far less brilliant. This is one of the hardiest of the barbs.

The Black Ruby Barb *(Puntius nigrofasciatus)* grows to about 2½ inches in length and is also brilliant when spawning. The male's colors range from deep red at the nose to jet black at the tail.

The Two-spot Barb *(Puntius ticto)* is not a well-colored fish but is nevertheless popular. It grows to about 2½ inches in length, and its large scales shine with reflected light. The dorsal fin of the male is trimmed with red, and this color becomes intense during breeding.

Cherry Barb (5); Rosy Barb (6); Black Ruby Barb (7); Two-spot (8)

female

male

1

2

male

female

male

3

female

Breeding danios and barbs

Generally speaking, breeding danios and barbs is easy and can be accomplished by most aquarists with a little experience and patience. Rasboras are difficult and should be left to the expert.

Danios and barbs spawn in a similar manner, although they lay different types of egg and an individual set-up is required for each. When a male and a female are placed together, the male will start courting his mate by swimming around her with his fins spread to their fullest. This usually impresses the female and she will respond by following him around. They will start to nudge one another until they both become very excited. Then, swimming side by side they tremble and the female releases eggs as the male releases sperm. The eggs immediately absorb water and sperm and are fertilized. This process continues until the female has released all her eggs and at this point it is best to remove both fish. Through their exertions they will have developed a hearty appetite, and they will quickly make a meal of the eggs they have just produced if left in the breeding tank.

The eggs take from one to four days to hatch, according to species. On hatching, the fry look like small slivers of glass hanging around the tank. If a magnifying glass is used it will be seen that these fry still have a large yolk sac, and it takes an additional day or two of development before this disappears and the fish are swimming freely. At this stage, food is required in the form of infusoria (minute organisms) for two or three days followed by brine shrimp until the fry can take small cyclops and *Daphnia*. The practice of rearing fish on nothing but fine, dry food is not to be recommended.

It is surprising how often aquarists' attempts to breed a particular species of fish have been unsuccessful because of the amazing fact that the fish involved were not even a pair. An amateur is recommended to purchase at least half a dozen healthy young fish. As they develop, a close watch will reveal the sex differences and a true pair can be obtained.

Pairs of Cherry Barbs (*Capoeta titteya*) (1), Zebra Danios (*Brachydanio rerio*) (2) and Leopard Danios (*Brachydanio frankei*) (3) showing sex differences

When an attempt at breeding is to be made, it is best to segregate the sexes for a period of a week or two and to feed the fish as rich and varied a diet as possible to bring them to the peak of condition. During this period, the spawning tank can be prepared. As both danios and barbs will readily eat their own spawn, some sort of protection is necessary. The eggs of the danios do not adhere to material objects, as do some. A breeding trap made of plastic mesh of the type suggested for the live-bearers is therefore recommended. This should be fairly large in order to allow plenty of swimming space. A simpler method, however, is to wash and clean a 16-inch × 8-inch × 8-inch tank and cover the bottom with a layer of marbles or pebbles previously sterilized by boiling. Water should then be added to provide 2 to 3 inches of swimming depth. Fresh water should be used, but the pH and hardness are of no real importance. The temperature should be around 80° F. A pair of fish placed in this tank one evening usually spawn the next morning and should be removed once the spawning is completed.

Arrangement of breeding tank for barbs

soft acid water

weighted breeding mop

water at 80°F

A layer of pebbles in the breeding tank will prevent danios from eating their eggs.

After spawning the fish will be tired, and the female especially will be much slimmer. The eggs, when laid, will drop to the bottom and fall into the crevices where the fish cannot find them. Water of the same temperature should now be added to almost fill the tank so that the fry have plenty of room when they hatch.

The eggs of the barbs are slightly adhesive and therefore need modified provisions. The tank size also needs to be larger —at least 18 inches × 10 inches × 10 inches. This should be filled with fairly soft (100 ppm) and slightly acid (pH 6.6–6.8) water. At one end, large clumps of sterilized coconut fiber or nylon mops should be placed so that the fish will be attracted to that end to spawn. The whole tank can be loosely filled with coconut fiber just as effectively. The fish spawn in and over this medium and can, of course, eat any eggs visible if not removed once spawning has finished.

When the fry of both types are free swimming, they will need a lot of food, although care must be taken not to overfeed or pollution may occur. Mild aeration will help to prevent the danger of pollution.

Gourami (*Osphronemus goramy*)

Exposed gill chamber of a labyrinth fish to show the labyrinth organ

labryinth organ

gill arch

Family Anabantidae (labyrinth fish)

There are over 38 species of labyrinth fish known to aquarists, in sizes ranging from 1½ inches to 2 feet. The distinctive feature of members of this family is the possession of a special respiratory organ which allows the fish to breathe atmospheric air.

The labyrinth organ consists of concentrically arranged bony plates with a vascular membrane enclosed in an enlarged gill cavity. The fish comes to the surface and takes in a mouthful of air, which is then forced into the labyrinth where gaseous exchange occurs. This labyrinth organ allows the Anabantidae to live in oxygen-poor water and to survive longer in polluted tanks in which other fish will die. However, anabantids are not really suitable for the community tank as they tend to bully other fish.

Varieties Cambodia (*above*) and
Blue Fighting Fish (*below*)

The Siamese Fighting Fish *(Betta splendens)* from south-east Asia is a beautiful and easily kept fish and the first egg-layer a beginner should attempt to breed. In the wild it lives in ponds and irrigation ditches. The male is extremely aggressive toward other males, and in Thailand fights are staged between male fighting fish very much as cock fighting used to be in the West. This fish requires no special pH or hardness of water but prefers a shallow tank containing some plants. The tank should be in a well-lighted position and have a temperature of 72°–82° F. Adult males cannot be kept together, but one male and a few females do well together in a community tank. The fins of the female are always small and unimposing, whereas those of the male are well-developed and magnificently flowing.

Adult male (*left*) and female (*right*) *Betta splendens*

Breeding Siamese Fighting Fish

A male and female must first be selected and conditioned separately, being given plenty of live foods. It is recommended that the bottom of the breeding tank be painted black on the outside and that it contain no gravel. The male should be put into the tank in the evening and later a jar containing the female can be introduced. Next morning, when the female is gently turned out of the jar, the male will begin to court her.

During courtship the male chases the female and swims alongside her, extending his gill covers and fins. He then begins to blow a bubble-nest among the floating plants [1]. The bubbles adhere, and a nest up to four inches in diameter and half an inch above the surface may be built. When the

Breeding tank with floating weed suitable for 'fighters'

nest is completed, the male drives the female up under it, she turns over on her side and he wraps himself around her [2]. She releases a few eggs and these are fertilized as both fish drift slowly downward. The male then picks up the eggs in his mouth and blows them into the nest. This process is repeated until the female is empty of eggs. At this stage the male becomes aggressive toward the female, and if she is not removed he will almost certainly kill her.

The male tends to the eggs until the fry hatch [3]. Some fall out and spiral away to the bottom but are picked up and blown back by the male. After about five days the fry are free swimming and the male should then be removed. The fry should be fed with infusoria or fine egg yolk for a few days and then given freshly hatched brine shrimp. Later, micro-worm, screened *Daphnia* and chopped whiteworm can be given.

Not every attempt to spawn 'fighters' may be successful; young fish may eat their eggs, or the male may not look after them after hatching. The fish should be reconditioned and put together about a month later.

Newly hatched 'fighter'

85

Popular labyrinth fish

The Climbing Perch *(Anabas testudineus)* is not a perch and does not really climb. It can, however, use its tail to 'walk' several hundred yards on land from one stretch of water to another, propped up on its pectoral fins and gill covers. During these excursions the fish uses its labyrinth organ to breathe moist air.

Unlike most labyrinth fish the male of the Javan Mouth-breeding Fighting Fish *(Betta brederi)* incubates the eggs in its mouth. They hatch after two days and are released after five days, by which time they are free swimming.

The Honey Gourami *(Colisa chunae)* is a small fish just over 1¼ inches in length. The male builds a nest which may cover a large area of the tank. Spawning is similar to the Siamese Fighting Fish but the eggs float and at 80° F hatch in 24 hours.

The dorsal and caudal fins in both sexes of the Comb-tail Paradise Fish *(Belontia signata)* have extensions or

Climbing Perch (1); Java Mouth-breeding Fighting Fish (2); Honey Gourami (3); Comb-tail Paradise Fish (4)

Paradise Fish (5a); mutant albino form (5b)

filaments, giving the appearance of the teeth of a comb. This fish, which originated in Ceylon, can be rather boisterous. The nest is very flimsy and may consist of only a few well-dispersed bubbles among the floating plants. The eggs float and hatch in two days. Parents should be removed or, alternatively, the eggs can be spooned off into a separate container, immediately after spawning.

The Paradise Fish *(Macropodus opercularis)* comes from the Far East and was probably the first tropical aquarium fish. It is a very hardy fish and can be kept outdoors in garden pools in summer in the warmer parts of the country. It grows to 4 inches in length, and the male is more highly colored and has larger fins than the female. These fish can be kept at 60°– 70° F, though raising the temperature to 78° F stimulates spawning. The spawning procedure is very similar to that of the Siamese Fighting Fish. Occasional specimens can be pugnacious, especially toward smaller fish and must be introduced into the community aquarium with care.

A mutant albino form sometimes occurs and is very popular among many aquarists.

male

female

A pair of Dwarf Gouramis

The Dwarf Gourami (*Colisa lalia*) is a very colorful member of the labyrinth family and grows up to 2 inches long. A peaceful, hardy fish, but very shy, it tends to hide among the plants and to come out only for food. For breeding purposes it is important to choose males with unbroken, and as near perfectly matching transverse bars as possible. About eight young fish are usually reared together in a well-planted tank. After a while the males develop their breeding colors and the females get very plump. The selected pair should be placed in an 18-inch × 10-inch × 10-inch tank with a water depth of 4 inches and the top covered with various floating plants. No gravel is needed. The temperature should be slowly raised to between 78°–82° F and before long the male will build a bubble nest, reinforced with small pieces of plant, and spawning will occur. It is advisable to remove the female immediately, but the male can be left until the eggs hatch. About 200 eggs are laid in a good spawning, and they hatch within 36 to 48 hours. They are very small and should be fed infusoria.

At about two weeks they are ready to eat brine shrimp and micro-worm. If 50 fry reach maturity the aquarist has done very well.

The Kissing Gourami (*Helostoma temmincki*) from southeast Asia is yelowish-orange silvery color all over. These fish have the habit of 'kissing' each other with everted lips.

The Chocolate Gourami (*Sphaerichthys osphromenoides*) is a difficult fish to keep in the aquarium and there are conflicting reports on its requirements. The Chocolate Gourami is reported as a mouth-brooder.

The Pearl or Mosaic Gourami (*Trichogaster leeri*) originated in southeast Asia. Immature fish are difficult to sex but, when mature, the female has a more rounded dorsal fin and is plump. The male builds a large bubble nest.

The very common Three-spot Gourami (*Trichogaster trichopterus trichopterus*) can grow up to 6 inches in length. These fish are easy to spawn and they breed in the usual anabantid way, the male constructing a bubble-nest.

Kissing Gourami (1); Chocolate Gourami (2); Pearl Gourami (3); Three-spot Gourami (4)

Distribution of the characins

Family Characidae (characins)

Members of this family form one of the largest freshwater fish families in the world. There are about 100 species available to the aquarist, and there is considerable variation among them. As will be seen from the above map, the world distribution of this family is restricted to the African and American continents, but the percentage of aquarium fish from Africa is very low. The Amazon basin of South America with its maze of waterways and streams is continually providing new species as scientists probe further inland. As yet, vast areas are still unexplored and will undoubtedly provide numerous specimens suitable for the aquarium.

All characins possess either teeth or an adipose fin and very often they have both. The adipose is a small, nearly transparent fin situated on the back of the fish just in front of the caudal and can be called the 'trademark' of the characins. Members of this family like live foods in variety but will also take dry foods quite readily.

Characins come in all shapes and sizes and therefore suit all tastes. Specimens vary in length from one inch to over one foot and from long and slender to flat and compressed. Some species like a small proportion of vegetable matter in their diet and if this is insufficiently provided, they will play havoc with plants. The majority of the smaller species are peaceful fish and suitable for the community aquarium, but the larger fish are more aggressive.

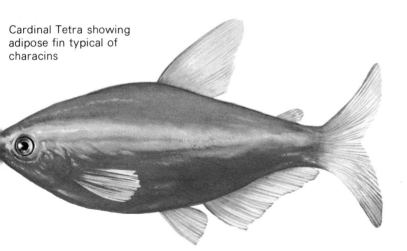

Cardinal Tetra showing
adipose fin typical of
characins

Some species are easily bred, others are extremely difficult. Some of the popular species fall into this latter class, and as a result their prices remain high. Quite a number of the species from South America are known as tetras, and one of the most common is the Neon Tetra *(Hyphessobrycon innesi)* (see page 101). It is doubtful if any other fish has been described in print more frequently and most aquarists dream of one day spawning some of these beautiful fish. Professional breeders have mastered the art as the fish can be purchased reasonably and are always in good supply. Unfortunately, the Neon Tetra is susceptible to a disease 'plistophora' or 'neon disease', which appears as a whitish patch on the body beneath the dorsal fin. No cure is known and as it is suspected of being contagious, infected fish should be killed immediately.

In 1956 in the United States, a fish with even brighter colors than the Neon Tetra made its first appearance and was named *Hyphessobrycon cardinalis.* Later this was changed to *Cheirodon axelrodi,* but its popular name of the Cardinal Tetra still remains. To date this fish has defied mass production techniques and its price is high. Shaded tanks, containing soft acid water, are essential to the well-being of all the characins. Other characins of the genus *Hyphessobrycon* are described on the following pages. This genus is popular with many aquarists, as the fish are colorful, hardy and quite undemanding. They are somewhat difficult to breed, however.

Lemon Tetra

Rosy Tetra

Bleeding Heart Tetra

Hyphessobrycon serpae

The Lemon Tetra *(Hyphessobrycon pulchripinnis)* is an old favorite although not brilliantly colored. It grows to 2 inches in length and can be spawned fairly easily. Plants should be provided in the breeding tank, however, to reduce the chances of the eggs being eaten.

The Rosy, or Black Flag, Tetra *(Hyphessobrycon rosaceus)* is one of the most beautiful characins. The males have longer dorsal and anal fins than the females. These fish prefer soft, acid water and look their best in subdued light in a school. They are somewhat difficult to spawn.

The Bleeding Heart Tetra *(Hyphessobrycon rubrostigma)* is similar to *H. rosaceus* but larger and not as colorful. It grows to 3 inches in length but is not too easy to keep and relatively difficult to spawn.

Hyphessobrycon serpae is very similar to *H. callistus* but smaller and a brighter red in color. The shoulder marking is a small dot. Like all the red-colored characins, these fish look their best in a school. This is one of the more beautiful small aquarium fish but not often seen. It is a restful, quiet fish.

The Bentos Tetra (*Hyphessobrycon bentosi*) is not very common at present but is becoming more popular. It grows to about 1½ inches in length and is closely related to *H. callistus*.

The body color of *Hyphessobrycon callistus* is pale red and the fins are black. The fish has a black vertical bar on the shoulder and measures about 1½ inches in length. This fish is very similar to *H. serpae*, with which it is sometimes confused.

The Red, or Flame, Tetra (*Hyphessobrycon flammeus*) rarely lives up to its name. Possibly as a result of continuous line breeding, the red color has paled to a rose tint in most fish. However, this tetra is very undemanding and breeding is easy, even in hard water. For small fish, they are long-lived, usually surviving for three to four years. The recommended temperature range for the species is 70°–80° F.

The Black Neon (*Hyphessobrycon herbertaxelrodi*) was introduced to aquarists in the early 1960's and in soft, acid water is really quite attractive. Males are about 1¼ inches long and females about 1¾ inches, which makes distinguishing the sexes easier.

Bentos Tetra

Hyphessobrycon callistus

Red Tetra

Black Neon

93

Hemigrammus ocellifer

The characins of the genus *Hemigrammus* also originated in South America, from the Amazon basin. *Hemigrammus ocellifer,* commonly known as either the Beacon Fish or the Head-and-Tail-Light Fish, is not a brilliant fish but when settled in an aquarium it produces bright splashes of color. The spot in the base of the caudal fin glows golden and the top half of the eye is golden red. The tips of all the fins have a splash of white. Sex can often be determined before the fish are adult, as the males have a faint white bar crossing the anal fin. At maturity, the females are larger and plumper than the males.

The more recent introduction of *Hemigrammus ocellifer ocellifer,* with extra black and gold spots on the flanks, has replaced the original fish somewhat and as they are easily bred, they are always available. Where possible, at least half a dozen should be purchased as they are more attractive in a school. This fish seems to be more susceptible than most to

Hemigrammus ocellifer ocellifer

the white spot disease, so extra care should be taken when purchasing.

The Glowlight Tetra *(Hemigrammus erythrozonus)* has caused a lot of confusion over its name. Sometimes it is known as *Hemigrammus gracilis,* and it has even been placed in the genus *Hyphessobrycon.*

The fish can be overlooked in the dealer's brightly lit tanks because the body is often pale and the line along the body faded to a dull orange. Tetras do not like strong light as a rule, and the Glowlight is no exception. However, if kept in a well-planted and moderately lighted aquarium the body becomes a soft, translucent brown and the line turns bright red.

male

female

An adult pair of Glowlight Tetras

A splash of red appears in the base of both the dorsal and anal fins and all the fins have white tips.

Not many years ago, this fish was expensive as it was not easy to breed, but it is now one of the cheapest fish and can be spawned quite easily if the right conditions are provided. Glowlights grow to about only 1¾ inches in length and do not like the company of larger fish. As with the Beacon Fish, at least half a dozen should be purchased and introduced to a tank containing other small fish, preferably characins. Adult males are slightly smaller and slimmer than the adult females.

male

A pair of Spraying Characins (*top* and *bottom*)

The Spraying Characin *(Copeina arnoldi)* has one unusual claim to fame—its method of reproduction. To protect its eggs from underwater predators, this fish lays them on some object, usually overhanging vegetation, about an inch above the surface. The pair of spawning fish move toward the surface and then together leap clear of the water, clinging long enough to the spawning ground to lay and fertilize a few eggs. They then drop back into the water and repeat the exercise until they have laid up to one hundred eggs. At this point the male takes over, driving the female away. The spawning site in the wild may be a large leaf or plant stem, but in a half-filled aquarium, a long piece of slate protruding above the water a few inches is acceptable to the fish.

For three or four days the eggs remain above the surface, and during this period the male periodically sprays water onto the spawn to keep it moist. This he does by rapidly moving his tail just beneath the surface of the water underneath the eggs. The fry drop into the water on hatching, and at this stage the parents should be removed.

Another characin with an unusual spawning method is

female

male

A pair of Swordtail Characins (*top* and *bottom*)

the Swordtail Characin (*Corynopoma riisei*),and even now experts are not certain what actually takes place.

The male, apart from having extensions on some of its fins, including the lower part of the tail, has long filaments extending from the gill covers at the end of which are small discs. Normally these gill extensions lie flat along the body of the fish, but when the courtship display takes place they are extended at right angles. How fertilization of the eggs takes place is a mystery, as the fish do not come together during spawning. They swim side by side a short distance apart and a few seconds later the female deposits eggs on a plant leaf. The whole process is repeated several times until about one hundred eggs are laid.

Whether internal fertilization takes place is not certain, but it has been reported that females separated from males for some time have produced eggs which have hatched. Some breeders think that the male ejects sperm into the spoon-like discs on the gill filaments and then transfers this to the female. Others think that the female carries sperm in her mouth as she pecks at the leaves before depositing the eggs.

female

Other members of the Characidae
The White, or Spotted, Piranha *(Serrasalmus rhombeus)*, the so-called 'terror of the Amazon', has extremely powerful and sharp teeth. It is reputed to be capable of stripping the flesh from a cow in a few minutes.

The Red Piranha *(Rooseveltiella nattereri)* grows to 12 inches in the wild. There are a number of genera to which the popular name piranha is given. A number of species have been kept and bred in aquaria in recent years, but in general only young fish are suitable for private aquaria.

Metynnis schreitmuelleri is closely related to the piranhas but has completely different characteristics. It requires a mixed diet in the aquarium with some vegetable matter.

The X-ray Fish *(Pristella riddlei)* is attractive, easily bred and a fish every beginner should have. Males are distinguished by a white line on the leading edge of the anal fin.

White Piranha (1); *Metynnis schreitmuelleri* (2); Red Piranha (3); X-ray Fish (4)

Nannostomus anomalus is a small example of the pencil-fish which is easily obtainable although not too popular. It does not display itself well in dealers' tanks, but retires to the shady corners it prefers. It is relatively easy to breed.

The Emperor Tetra *(Nematobrycon palmeri)* is one of the most beautiful of the tropical fish. The males are distinguished by tail extensions. It is not a prolific breeder.

The Congo Tetra *(Micralestes interruptus)* is one of the

Nannostomus anomalus (5); Emperor Tetra (6); Congo Tetra (7); *Neolebias ansorgei* (8)

few worthwhile characins from Africa. It is rarely seen but worth purchasing should be the opportunity arise.

The colors of *Neolebias ansorgei* really shine in the very soft acid water it prefers. It is easily bred but is a shy fish, tending to hide in vegetation.

Soft water is essential for breeding characins and can be collected as rain water as shown. All surfaces should be plastic, if possible, to avoid contamination.

Breeding characins

In most cases, breeding characins is much more of a problem than breeding barbs and danios. Generally speaking, however, characins spawn in the same manner as the barbs, in that the male courts the female and eventually both fish come together side by side and fertilized eggs are released. Here the similarity ends. Characin eggs usually hatch more quickly and the fry are much smaller than those of the barbs. It is not unusual to have a pair of fish spawn in the morning and to see the fry hatched later the same day. Of course, they are very poorly developed at first and will not require food for some days. Because they are smaller, the fry should be fed on infusoria for longer than is necessary for barbs, although it is surprising how large the mouth of the fry is in proportion to body size.

Water conditions are extremely important. A few species such as the Black Widow, or Black Tetra *(Gymnocorymbus ternetzi)*, the Beacon Fish *(Hemigrammus ocellifer)* and the Black-line Tetra *(Hyphessobrycon scholzei)* can be persuaded to spawn in water with a hardness of 150–180 ppm and with pH on the alkaline side, but with the Neon Tetra *(Hyphessobrycon innesi)* and some others the pH must be lower at about 6, but most important, the hardness must be below 15 ppm.

If tap water is soft, it is only necessary to leave it standing for a short while to allow any chlorine to dissipate. Hard tap water, however, must be 'softened'. This is done by passing it through a commercial water softener which exchanges the calcium and magnesium salts for sodium, but this 'soft' water is not recommended for breeding, although it can be used in a community aquarium. For the aquarist with hard tap water the collection of rain water is therefore a necessity. Rain water collected in the country can be used within a few days. In town, however, the rain has absorbed atmospheric impurities and these must be allowed to settle out or evaporate. It is a good idea to allow this rain water to 'mature' over a layer of well-boiled peat to produce suitable water for characins.

The brilliantly colored Neon Tetra is difficult to spawn

When breeding fish such as the Zebra Danio bright light acts as a stimulus, but with characins it has the reverse effect. It is therefore advisable to place the breeding tank where it will not receive strong light, and after the fish have spawned, the tank should be covered completely so that as little light as possible enters. It is possible that strong light produces either too much, or a special type of bacteria which attacks the eggs, but this is not certain. The breeding tank can have some of its sides painted to exclude light, but this seems to have a claustrophobic effect on the fish if a small aquarium is used. The water temperature should be around 80° F, and a nylon breeding mop should be included as the eggs are adhesive or semi-adhesive.

Very often characins do not spawn on the day after they have been placed in the breeding tank, and there is always a temptation to feed the fish. This should not be done and fish can generally last at least a week without being fed. Feeding results in uneaten food and more excreta, producing bacteria harmful to the eggs when the fish do spawn.

Breeding tank with nylon mop suitable for the smaller characins. Painted sides help to exclude light.

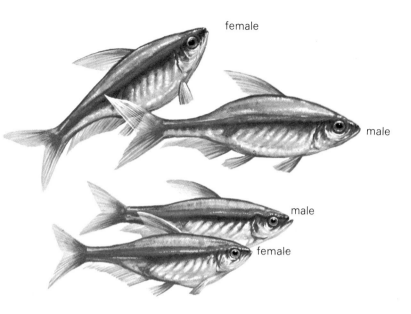

female

male

male

female

Glowlight Tetras perform an unusual 'barrel-roll' during spawning. During the movement, which takes place extremely quickly, the female moves over and around the male while releasing her eggs. The pair then separate and repeat the movement until spawning is complete.

It is impossible to exclude all bacteria as the breeding fish are bound to produce some excreta while in the tank, but it is very important to keep the bacteria level to a minimum. If the spawning tank is well washed before it is set up, the water well-matured over peat and the spawning medium boiled before it is placed in the aquarium, then the conditions should be suitable.

The fry of the characins are also very light-conscious and when the eggs do hatch, the breeder should not be surprised if he sees nothing during the day. Quite a few eggs may turn white due to infertility, while the fry that hatch have a tendency to go into hiding. The best way to see if anything has happened is to wait until after dark and then shine a bright light into the tank from the side and look in from the top. The fry, which have by this time moved around the tank, immediately dive for cover. After a week or so, the fish will be a little braver and will move into open water, but even at this stage they are still very shy.

Family Cichlidae (cichlids)

In the wild, cichlids live in standing or sluggish water with good hiding places under overhanging banks or among plants. They take up definite territories, the boundaries of which are fiercely defended, and characteristic attack, defense and surrender postures have been well described. In groups of aquarium cichlids a hierarchy in order of aggressiveness often becomes established — a 'pecking order'.

Apart from *Tilapia* and *Geophagus* species, which are almost completely vegetarian, the cichlids are carnivorous and feed on smaller fish and aquatic insects in their natural environment. Dried food will be eaten if nothing else is provided but minced liver, fish and cod roe are acceptable substitutes for live foods. A number of species enjoy digging up the gravel, thus uprooting plants, and are therefore better kept in a tank set up especially for them. Although most cichlids are not particular about the pH or hardness of water, most species do better if kept in soft, acid water.

Because of their relatively large size and quick growth under the right conditions, cichlids are used as food fish in many tropical regions of the world. Young fish are placed in rice paddies and then harvested when the rice is picked (see page 5).

To breed cichlids it is often better to let eight to twelve young fish grow up together and let them choose their own mates as they become sexually mature. There have been instances where the male has refused to mate with, and in

Distribution of the cichlids

Typical cichlid spawning
behavior

some cases even killed, an apparently suitable female newly
introduced to the tank.

In a typical spawning the partners select a flat stone or
broad plant leaf and clean it to their satisfaction [1]. Dwarf
cichlids need clean, clear, soft acid water with no gravel and
find a plant-pot a good substitute for a flat stone. When courtship begins, both fish become vividly colored. The female lays
her eggs in regular rows on the stone, a few at a time, and
these are immediately fertilized by the male [2]. Usually both
parents (sometimes only one) then stand guard over the eggs,
fanning them and picking out infertile ones [3]. When the eggs
hatch, usually two days later, the fry are moved by the parents
to another spot and guarded there until they are free swimming,
usually in three to five days. Even then the fry are kept together in a school and protected by the parents [4]. In the
mouth-breeders, the fertilized eggs are carried about in the
mouth of one or the other parent until the fry are free swimming.

About 20 of the 60 species of cichlids available to the aquarist are under four inches in length and are known as dwarf cichlids. More demanding in their needs than the larger cichlids, they must have soft acid water for spawning. The female usually looks after the brood after hatching, and the male should be removed after spawning has taken place. One variety, Agassiz's Dwarf Cichlid (*Apistogramma agassizi*), comes from the Amazon Basin.

Ramirez' Dwarf Cichlid (*Apistogramma ramirezi*) is a very beautiful fish. To keep it in its best condition the water must be soft and acid and absolutely clean.

The Golden-eyed Dwarf Cichlid (*Nannacara anomala*) comes from Guiana and is relatively easy to breed. After spawning, the male should be removed. The female will then move the newly hatched fish to a hollow in the gravel, where they become free swimming on the fifth day after hatching.

Pelmatochromis kribensis comes from West Africa and is one of the larger dwarf cichlids. These fish are great diggers and will dig a pit in the gravel two inches deep

Agassiz's Dwarf Cichlid

Ramirez' Dwarf Cichlid

Golden-eyed Dwarf Cichlid

Pelmatochromis kribensis

Keyhole Cichlid

Blue Acara

Marbled Cichlid

Jack Dempsey

and three inches across very easily. The broods often tend to contain many more fish of one sex than the other.

Some members of the Cichlidae are not very popular as they grow large, grub up plants and need plenty of live foods. The Keyhole Cichlid (*Aequidens maroni*), however, is a peaceful fish in which parental care is usually very good. The sex difference is most easily seen in the more pointed dorsal and anal fins of the male.

The Blue Acara (*Aequidens pulcher*), although a very beautiful fish, grows too large for the average aquarist. The best specimens are to be seen in the large tanks of public aquaria.

The Marbled or Velvet Cichlid (*Astronotus ocellatus*) grows to 13 inches in length, but even at this size it is a peaceful fellow. The young fish, up to 6 inches long, are much prettier than the adults, whose marbled effect is less bright and which are more heavy in shape.

The Jack Dempsey (*Cichlasoma biocellatum*) is an aptly named fish. A predator, growing to 8 inches in length, it is destructive to plants and not a suitable species for the community tank.

Fire-mouth Cichlid (1); Banded Cichlid (2); *Geophagus jurupari* (3); Pike Cichlid (4)

The Fire-mouth Cichlid *(Cichlasoma meeki)* is a popular cichlid, probably because it is peaceful, well-behaved and easy to breed. A mature pair in good condition will often breed in the community tank, the parents taking turns either to guard the eggs or to patrol to keep intruders out.

The Banded Cichlid *(Cichlasoma severum)* is another attractive cichlid to keep, but it is more likely to dig up plants than is the Fire-mouth. This is an easy fish to breed once a pair decide they are compatible, but the male may be possessive and behave aggressively toward strange females.

The Pike Cichlid *(Crenicichla lepidota)* is a predatory fish with a big mouth. Because of its predatory nature, it requires a tank to itself.

Geophagus jurupari, sometimes called the Earth-eating Devilfish, is the most peaceful of the 'earth eaters' available to aquarists. The name 'earth eater' originates from the thorough way in which it digs up the bottom of the aquarium.

The Orange Chromide *(Etroplus maculatus)* comes from India and Ceylon, often from brackish water. Orange Chromides spawn in the usual cichlid manner and both parents look after the fry. Often, however, it is better to remove both parents and aerate the eggs artificially.

The Small or Egyptian Mouth-breeder *(Haplochromis multicolor)* is a popular aquarium fish. After spawning in excavations in the gravel, the female takes all the eggs in her mouth where they hatch after ten days.

The Red or Jewel Cichlid *(Hemichromis bimaculatus)* is one of the most beautiful and interesting of cichlids. Often too robust for community tanks, they live quite well among their own kind. Spawning takes place on a flat stone with both fish taking care of the eggs. The young need plenty of live food or much destructive fin biting will occur.

The Mozambique Cichlid or Mouth-brooder *(Tilapia mossambica)* is a representative of a large genus of cichlids from Africa; many of these fish are used as foods. The eggs are laid in shallow depressions and are immediately taken into the mouth of the female where they hatch after ten days.

Orange Chromide (5); Mozambique Cichlid (6); Small Mouth-breeder (7); Jewel Cichlid (8)

1

2

3   4

5   6

110

7   8

The angelfish (*Pterophyllum* sp.) are native to the Amazon and the Orinoco and are the most popular of all cichlids. There are three species: *P. altum, P. eimekei* and *P. scalare*, and the differences between them are recognizable only by the expert. Many of the 'angels' in fish tanks today are probably hybrids from the latter two species. They are peaceful fish, very suitable for the community tank, but should not be kept below 74° F. They seem to do best in slightly acid water at a pH of 6.8.

Angelfish are best left to choose mates for themselves. Once they have selected each other a pair will proceed to clean up one of the leaves of a broad-leafed plant, the eggs are then laid and looked after by both parents. Many aquarists prefer to let them spawn on a piece of slate, which is then removed and put near an aerator until the eggs hatch. Immature fish are impossible to sex. They do, however, exhibit the typical cichlid rather than angel shape until they are three or four weeks old. Young fish will eat powder-fine dried food, but it is not as good for them as live food.

The Discus *(Symphysodon discus)* is a particularly spectacular aquarium fish, the breeding color of which rival the gaudy beauty of most marine fish. This is probably the fish most aquarists would like to be able to rear successfully. It is a difficult fish to keep and needs clean, very soft, acid water. It appears to do much better if the water is regularly filtered through a filter containing peat. All live foods are accepted by the Discus but when young fish are first bought it is sometimes difficult to persuade them to feed.

Spawning takes place in the usual cichlid way, on plant leaves or stones, and both parents share in 'fanning' the eggs. The young hatch in about two days and are transferred to leaves onto which they hang for another two days before becoming free swimming. The parents at this stage appear to secrete a nutritious substance from the skin on which the young feed for a few days. With good care they grow rapidly to 3 or 4 inches in six months. Growth then slows down, and it takes about two to three years for a fish to reach 6 inches.

Angelfish (1, 3) with young (2), and Discus (5, 6) showing color varieties (4, 7, 8)

Spiny Catfish (1); Bronze Catfish (2); *Pimelodella* (3); Whiptail Catfish (4)

Other interesting species

The Bronze Catfish *(Corydoras aeneus)* is the most common member of a very large genus from South America. All members have the same body shape, but the body patterns vary quite a lot. Sizes range from 1¼ to 3½ inches in length.

Pimelodella gracilis is another catfish from South America, having long whiskers. These fish grow to at least 6 inches long and are therefore suitable for only the largest aquaria.

Acanthodoras spinosissimus is known as the Spiny or Talking Catfish, the latter because it makes a croaking noise at times. It is not a pretty fish. Its fins are very stiff and spiny and it grows to at least 5 inches in length.

The Whiptail Catfish *(Loricaria parva)* with its long, thin tail is aptly named. It likes algae in its diet, and it is therefore a useful fish for cleaning algae from rocks and glass in the aquarium. It has been successfully bred in captivity.

Otocinclus vittatus (5); *Plecostomus commersoni* (6); Glass Catfish (7); Upside-down Catfish (8)

Otocinclus vittatus is one of the more commonly seen algae eaters. Because of its size its appetite is not very large, and it should not be expected to clear too much algae. It reaches only 2 inches in length.

In contrast, *Plecostomus commersoni* will eat all the algae that can be provided, usually growing too big for the tank in the process. In nature it grows to well over a foot but fortunately does not reach that length in an aquarium. Because of its size it can damage plants when resting on them.

The Glass Catfish *(Kryptopterus bicirrhis)* is one of the most transparent fish seen in aquaria. Not really a scavenger like most catfish, it prefers live foods.

The Upside-down Catfish *(Synodontis nigriventris)* has the habit of swimming in an upside-down position for a while, returning to normal when at rest. There are one or two other species in the genus which have this peculiar habit.

The Kuhli Loach *(Acanthophthalmus kuhlii)* is common in most dealers' tanks, spending its time hiding in corners and under rocks. It moves very quickly, especially when a net comes close to it. It is an excellent scavenger.

The Clown Loach or Tiger Botia *(Botia macracantha)* is the most beautiful species of this genus. Not often seen, it is always expensive. Other species are imported from time to time and all make good scavengers.

Gyrinocheilus aymonieri is one of the most useful fish for the aquarist and nearly every tank should have one. It eats all the algae on the glass and plant leaves and does not grow too big. It has replaced *Plecostomus commersoni* as the most popular aquarium cleaner (see page 147).

Noemacheilus fasciatus is a little loach more interesting than the Kuhli Loach as it does not hide away so much. It is another excellent scavenger.

The Dwarf Rainbowfish *(Melanotaenia maccullochi)* is

Kuhli Loach (1); Clown Loach (2); *Gyrinocheilus aymonieri* (3); *Noemacheilus fasciatus* (4)

the most common member of the group of Australian rainbows. Interesting features are a double dorsal fin and the fact that they do not eat their eggs and can, therefore, be spawned very easily.

The Black-banded Sunfish *(Mesogonistius chaetodon)* is a native of the United States and does not like temperatures over about 70° F. It does not like dried foods and therefore can be difficult to keep.

The Malayan Angel or Fingerfish *(Mondactylus argenteus)* is one of the few fish kept in tropical aquaria which is really a brackish-water fish. As such, they appreciate some salt added to the water. They are shy fish and should be kept in a school if possible.

The Spotted Scat or Argus *(Scatophagus argus)* is similar to the previous species and inhabits the same waters. Scats look attractive in a tank with Malayan Angels and will eat all foods in huge quantities, including aquarium plants.

Dwarf Rainbowfish (5); Malayan Angel (6); Black-banded Sunfish (7); Scat (8)

The Spiny Eel (*Mastacembelus maculatis*) has a habit of burying itself in the gravel with only its eyes and snout showing. It is extremely difficult to catch when in the aquarium and is not really a fish for the community tank.

The Glassfish (*Chanda lala*) has a nearly transparent body and is quite hardy. It prefers hard water and live foods, although it will accept some dried foods. It is not easily bred and requires shallow water and plenty of plants.

The Butterfly-fish (*Pantodon buchholzi*), so named because of its large pectoral fins, has an enormous mouth and takes only live foods, mainly insects, at the surface. This is a freshwater flying fish, and is said to skim along the surface for distances up to six feet.

The Mudskipper (*Periophthalmus barbarus*) can and does spend a large part of its life out of water. When submerged it uses its extended eyes to look above the water before emerging. The pectoral fins are used as feet, and strong muscles enable these fish to move quickly when suddenly alarmed.

Spiny Eel (1); Glassfish (2); Butterfly-fish (3); Mudskipper (4)

The Common Puffer-fish (*Tetraodon cutcutia*) is a fish well known for its habit of inflating itself when alarmed. If the fish is taken from water, it usually performs this feat and remains floating upside-down for a few moments before deflating. These fish require some salt added to their aquarium and will eat most food. In the wild, they are scavengers.

The Bumblebee-fish (*Brachygobious xanthozona*) also appreciates a little salt in its water. These are timid fish and should be given a tank to themselves as they are slow to get to food. They will only eat live foods.

The African Knifefish (*Xenomystus nigri*) has no dorsal or caudal fins and swims by a rippling motion of the anal fin. It requires live food and is not a community fish.

The Archerfish (*Toxotes jaculator*) has a special mouth structure which enables it to expel small drops of water at insects on foliage, 3 or 4 feet above the water surface. It does this with extreme accuracy. This fish requires live food in the aquarium.

Common Puffer-fish (5); Bumble bee-fish (6); African Knifefish (7); Archerfish (8)

Although not the kind of fish every aquarist would want to keep, lungfish are biologically very interesting. They are 'living fossils', and their ancient ancestors were close to the ancestors of the amphibians 300 million years ago.

The primitive lungs of these fish enable them to breathe air, which is of great value in the dry season. Some species bury themselves in the mud as soon as the water dries up, forming a cocoon which keeps the fish moist. A hole at the mouth end of the cocoon allows the fish to breathe. This sleep ceases when the rains begin; the pools then fill with water again and the fish emerge from their cocoons. Other species of lungfish do not build cocoons but can live in small stagnant pools, breathing air to prevent asphyxiation.

In aquaria, lungfish always appear to be uninteresting, sluggish fish, sitting on the bottom of the tank. They eat fish, earthworms, meat snails and mussels. All species are capable of giving a nasty bite, so they must be handled with care. In the wild, breeding takes place at the beginning of the rainy season and the eggs are said to be large and yolky, like amphibian eggs. Most public Aquaria usually have at least one specimen of these unusual fish.

South American (1); African (2) and Australian (3) lungfish

Electric Catfish

Mention must be made of two other very interesting fish that are also more suitable for the public rather than the private aquarium. These fish can usually be seen in any of the larger public Aquaria.

The first fish is the Electric Catfish *(Malapterurus electricus)* which comes from Africa, and as its name suggests it is capable of discharging an electric current. As it grows to around 2 feet in length and lives exclusively on small, live fish few home aquariums are equipped to keep this fish. In many Aquaria, tanks containing these fish have electrical equipment to detect the discharges made by the fish. The results can be heard as a crackling noise on a loudspeaker.

The second unusual fish is *Arapaima gigas* (see page 7), one of the largest freshwater fish. These fish can reach 14 feet in length. It glides majestically around its tank by slight movements of the tail, paying no attention at all to other fish. Because of its shape, the Arapaima can move very fast when required. In the Amazon region this fish forms an important part of the diet of natives who dry the flesh and preserve it for future use.

FOODS AND FEEDING

All foodstuffs consist of varying amounts of the following substances: proteins, fats, carbohydrates, vitamins and mineral substances. Proteins, fats and carbohydrates are all capable of being used by the fish to give it energy, though fats have twice the calorific value of proteins and carbohydrates. Proteins are complex substances made up of amino acids. Some amino acids can be manufactured by the fish, but others called essential amino acids must come directly from the food which is eaten. Similarly, some of the fatty acids of which fats are composed cannot be manufactured from other fats by the fish and must be taken in as part of the diet. Vitamins are essential for growth and health, and supplies of minerals such as calcium, phosphorus and iodine must also be in adequate supply in order to prevent ill health and stunted growth.

To ensure healthy growth, therefore, the fish must have a mixed and balanced diet containing both dried food and various live foods such as whiteworm, *Tubifex, Daphnia,* earthworms and mosquito larvae. If there are algae or plants in the tank for the fish to eat, so much the better. This diet can be supplemented by protein foods such as liver, beef and heart to provide variety.

It must also be remembered that fish find some foods much more interesting than others, as do humans. Most fish, for example, would prefer to have their protein allowance in the form of living mosquito larvae rather than in pieces of cooked liver. Change helps to avoid boredom from one type of food, however.

There are some species which are more specialized in the way they like to take in their nutriment. The predators, for example, prefer living fish and insects while others prefer mainly plant food.

Of great use to the aquarist are the commercially prepared dried foods, generally consisting of a mixture of cereal, milk powder, prepared egg, dried *Daphnia,* shrimp or fish. These are dried and mixed together and presented as a fine powder or as flakes. Others have various chemicals added which are reputed to give color to the fish. The aquarist can prepare

Meat for aquarium fish can be shredded in a hand grinder.

his own dry food. Some, for example, grind down dry cat food to various sized particles. Others use various cereals, especially those in a flaky form prepared for babies, and our own experience is that these are very good. It is important to give dried foods in small quantities—no more than can be eaten by the fish in ten minutes. Any residue putrifies and will pollute the tank. More fish have died from this form of overfeeding than from underfeeding.

Fish can be given small pieces of cooked, flaked fish (especially when live food is scarce in winter), shrimp and small amounts of canned salmon. Liver is a particularly good food; it is high in protein, contains vitamins and is rich in iron. Raw liver, however, tends to make the tank cloudy; to avoid this the liver should be put in boiling water for a few minutes to coagulate the blood. The liver should then be cut into small cubes and shredded, in a blender or grinder. To improve this food, shrimp or cooked cod roe can also be shredded up in the blender and the whole lot mixed together.

Another useful food is a hard-boiled egg with the white removed. The yolk can be frozen in the refrigerator and bits sliced off when needed. From time to time fish also like a pinch of wheat germ, This contains large amounts of vitamin B and is liked very much by mollies.

A fine mesh nylon net can be used to collect water fleas and other live foods

121

Tubifex worms live in mud. They must be cleansed thoroughly before being fed to fish to avoid passing on bacterial infection.

A single *Tubifex* worm magnified. Actual worm about 1 inch long.

Whiteworms are related to earthworms. Cultures can be bought from pet shops.

Whiteworms

The whiteworm *(Enchytraeus albidus)* is one of the live foods that can be cultivated by the aquarist and so is available all the year round. To get a culture growing successfully a wooden box is required with provision for water to escape when the culture media is watered. Special culture media can be bought or mixtures of soil, peat and fine sand prepared at home and sterilized by heat before being used.

The worm culture is added to the moist culture medium and the food placed in a small hollow on top of the medium. A piece of glass is usually placed over the box and, finally, a lid. The box should be kept in the dark at about 55° F. The worms usually come up to the surface, eat the food and cling to the glass. They can easily be lifted off with forceps and fed to the fish.

Prepared food for whiteworms can be bought or, alternatively, baby cereal food can be used. After three days, any unused food should be removed and the whole culture medium stirred. This breaks up the medium, aerates it and improves the culture. Fish should not be fed whiteworms exclusively because they have a very high fat content and can cause obesity.

Tubifex

Tubifex worms live at the bottom of streams and rivers, particularly where large amounts of organic matter are present, as in polluted water. They have their front end buried in the mud and the rear end constantly waving in the water. If these worms are collected directly from a river it is difficult to avoid collecting smelly mud and the worms then need a lot of cleaning. It is, therefore, preferable to buy *Tubifex* from pet shops where they are already clean. Even so, the gut of the worm usually contains much organic matter and bacteria, and so the worms must be well washed for 48 hours before being fed to the fish. They are cleaned best by placing them in a bowl left under running water.

Because they are aquatic, *Tubifex* will continue to live in the gravel at the bottom of the tank if not eaten. They are very nutritious and well-liked by all fish. A recent development is freeze-dried *Tubifex* available from pet shops.

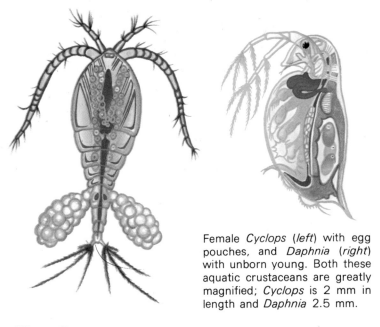

Female *Cyclops* (*left*) with egg pouches, and *Daphnia* (*right*) with unborn young. Both these aquatic crustaceans are greatly magnified; *Cyclops* is 2 mm in length and *Daphnia* 2.5 mm.

Water fleas

Water fleas form a large group of crustaceans living in ponds; the best known being *Daphnia* and *Cyclops*. These small creatures use their swimming antennae to move jerkily about in the water, and this is probably how the name 'flea' originated. They can be found in large numbers during the warm months of the year, especially if the pond contains rotting organic matter. Farmyard ponds are often very good sources of supply and the fleas should be caught by using a fine-mesh net and then fed quickly to the fish. During the summer, many young, usually females, are produced, but as the weather gets cooler resistant eggs which survive the winter are produced.

Because they feed predominantly on algae from which they obtain oil, *Daphnia* have a laxative property. They are, therefore, a very good food for fish kept in the confined space of an aquarium. It is wise not to overfeed, however, as a surfeit can kill the fish and may even pollute the tank.

Other live foods

Gnat or mosquito larvae are the larvae of *Culex pipiens* and are often found in enormous numbers on the surface of stagnant waters. Easily caught in the summer when catching

Daphnia, they are a nuisance because those that are uneaten hatch out as gnats in the fish house. Tooth-carps are particularly partial to gnat larvae. Some live-bearers have been used in mosquito control.

Bloodworms are the larvae of the midge *Chironomus plumosus.* They occur in large numbers in ponds and ditches receiving organic matter. If required in large numbers, they can be obtained by sieving mud from the upper layer of the pond bottom through a small sieve.

Glass or Phantom larvae are the transparent larvae of the fly *Corethra plumicornis.* They survive the winter in sheltered ponds. An excellent food, they are very hardy but should not be given alive to small fish because they have been known to eat spawn and newly hatched fry. They can be chopped or squashed for young fish.

The Freshwater Shrimp (*Gammarus pulex*) can be a useful food for larger fish as it grows to nearly an inch in length. Shrimp are often found under stones or among water plants in running water.

Examples of live foods for fish (magnified)

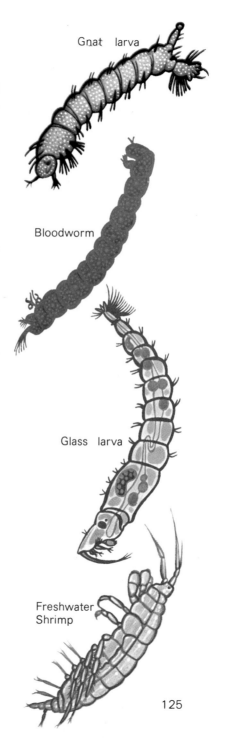

Gnat larva

Bloodworm

Glass larva

Freshwater Shrimp

Foods for fry

Many newly hatched fry have very small mouths and consequently need very small food for the first few days of life. Infusoria can be prepared by adding a small piece of bruised lettuce leaf to a small jar full of water. A small amount of aquarium water should be added to this and the mixture incubated at 76° F for 48 hours. The protozoa added with the tank water feed on the rotting lettuce leaf and multiply. A half jar twice a day of such infusoria should be sufficient for an average-sized aquarium.

Water from green tanks or ponds contains either *Euglena*

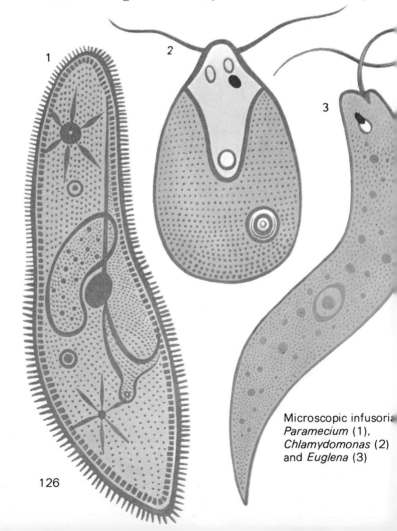

Microscopic infusoria
Paramecium (1),
Chlamydomonas (2)
and *Euglena* (3)

Micro-worms (*left*) and Brine Shrimp (*right*) are good foods for fry that have outgrown the need for infusoria

or *Chlamydomonas,* both excellent fry foods, which can also be cultured artificially. Newly hatched fry can also be fed on commercially available food which is easy to use. Another infusoria substitute is hard-boiled egg yolk which produces a cloud of very small nutritious particles in the breeding tank.

The Brine Shrimp *(Artemia salina)* is an important food for newly hatched fry with larger mouths. Brine Shrimp eggs are obtainable from most pet shops and can be hatched within 48 hours in a salt solution (two level teaspoonsful per pint of water) at 80° F. Using two or three small jars it is easy to organize a supply of newly hatched shrimp which can be filtered off through a very fine piece of cloth and rinsed into the tank.

Micro-worms *(Anguilluda silusia)* are small nematode worms only a fraction of an inch long. An initial culture must be obtained from another aquarist or pet shop. The culture medium consists of a one-inch layer of cooked oatmeal which has been allowed to cool in a four-inch diameter plastic dish. The culture should be placed on top of this layer and a lid placed over the dish before incubation at 70° — 80° F. The worms multiply rapidly and swarm up the sides of the box from which they can be removed with a small brush. The culture goes sour after a time and must be replaced by inoculating some new medium from the old culture.

Grindal worms *(Enchytraeus buchholtzi)* are similar to whiteworms and are very useful for feeding growing fry, as they grow to only ⅜-inch in length. Cultures of grindal worms can be bought from most dealers and pet shops.

127

transfer of infectio
to new tank on ne

infected fishes

infected fish

It is easy to spread an infectious disease from tank to tank. Quarantine-tank equipment should never be used in other tanks.

DISEASES OF FISH

Fish, like all animals, are subject to diseases, the most serious of which are infectious as these can wipe out a great many fish. Such diseases can, however, be cured, but prevention is a far better course of action.

Congenital diseases are diseases or deformities with which the fish is born, examples being missing gill covers and fins or twisted backbones. These deformities are usually genetic in origin and one should not use these fish for breeding again.

Traumatic diseases are produced by injuries, usually caused by other fish during fights or sometimes when the fish jump out when being netted.

Infectious diseases are tremendously common in fish tanks and are caused by protozoa, bacteria or viruses. Diseases caused by protozoa are the most common and the ones we know most about. All infectious diseases are introduced into a tank from another infected fish either directly, or by transferring the infection via a net. Many infectious diseases do not show at all in the early stages of development. The protozoa may be present on the fish but the characteristic lesion often does not develop. It can take up to six weeks before the illness becomes apparent, by which time other fish in the tank will have become infected.

Aquarists with only one tank rely on the source from which they get their fish being free of infection. Aquarists with several tanks should always have a quarantine tank with its own nets, feeding forceps and so on, which should never be used in other tanks. New fish, after a quarantine of six weeks, should be carefully examined in a good light before being placed with healthy fish.

Degenerative diseases are often caused by increasing age, and fish may develop heart failure, kidney failure which leads to dropsy, skeletal deformities, swim bladder and balance troubles. Neoplastic disease, namely cancers due to new growth and pigmented tumors, are not unknown in fish.

Healthy fish are easily recognized. They feed well, the fins are erect, they are active, their color is good and there are no spots or blemishes on the skin. Their eyes are bright and their gills pink. There are no skeletal deformities and the body cavity of the fish is not swollen or the belly hollow.

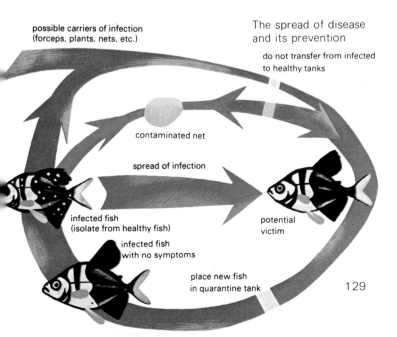

possible carriers of infection
(forceps, plants, nets, etc.)

The spread of disease
and its prevention

do not transfer from infected
to healthy tanks

contaminated net

spread of infection

infected fish
(isolate from healthy fish)

potential
victim

infected fish
with no symptoms

place new fish
in quarantine tank

129

White spot disease

This is the most common infectious disease seen in tropical aquaria and will kill fish if not checked. It is caused by a protozoan parasite *Ichthyophthirius multifilius,* and attacks are often caused by a drop in temperature of the aquarium water. The resistance of the fish becomes reduced and the vitality of the parasite increased. Diagnosis is not easy in the early stages of the disease when only one spot may be present on one fish. However, the parasite appears to cause an itching in infected fish and, in the early stages, fish may attempt to rub or scratch themselves against objects in the aquarium to reduce the irritation. The spots usually spread rapidly within a few days. As the life cycle of the parasite is known, control ·is not difficult.

The first step is to raise the water temperature to 82° F. This speeds up the development of the cysts to the free-living form, the stage at which a white spot preparation will kill the parasite. Such preparations are commercially prepared and sold at most pet shops. Instructions on the direction circular must be carefully followed.

Alternatively, the disease can be cured by using a five percent aqueous solution of methylene blue, available from all pharmacists. This is a very valuable substance to the aquarist as it also cures other diseases. Unfortunately, it harms plants so the fish must be put in an unplanted tank in which they

Black Molly infected with white spot disease

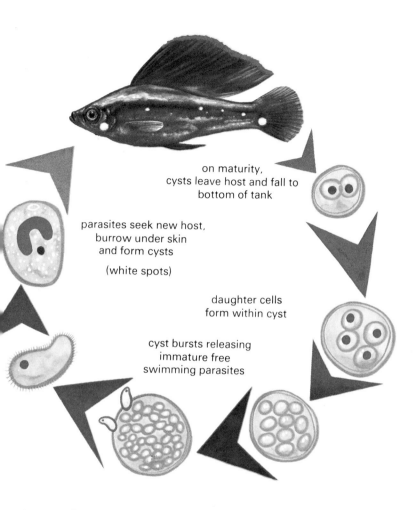

on maturity,
cysts leave host and fall to
bottom of tank

parasites seek new host,
burrow under skin
and form cysts

(white spots)

daughter cells
form within cyst

cyst bursts releasing
immature free
swimming parasites

Life cycle of the white spot parasite

must be kept for ten days. If the blue color of the water fades, more methylene blue should be added. The planted tank, without fish, will become free of parasites in ten days without any treatment.

If an outbreak of white spot disease occurs in a community tank, only certain species may become infected, due to several reasons. The parasite prefers certain species as hosts, some species can withstand chilling better than others, and certain fish in the aquarium will be in better health than others.

Velvet

This is a comparatively new disease among aquarium fish and affects mostly labyrinth fish and members of the carp family, such as the White Cloud Mountain Minnows, danios, barbs and also the live-bearing tooth-carps. Fish with velvet disease have golden dust-like spots on their skin as if sprayed with golden powder. If untreated, the condition of the fish deteriorates and a series of raised circular crusts develops. This condition is caused by the free-swimming form of

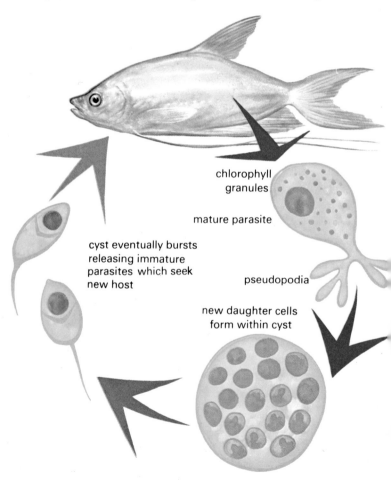

chlorophyll granules

mature parasite

cyst eventually bursts releasing immature parasites which seek new host

pseudopodia

new daughter cells form within cyst

Life cycle of the velvet parasite

Oodinium limneticum which adheres to the fish and grows pseudopodia into its skin to obtain nourishment. An infection usually kills young fish and fry usually succumb before the disease is suspected. The free-swimming form contains chlorophyll and can therefore exist for a long time in the presence of light without requiring a fish host. This means that it is a much more difficult parasite to get rid of than *Ichthyophthirius*.

All fish from the tank containing obviously infected fish must be put in an isolation tank and treated with methylene blue for ten days, as for white spot. Acriflavine (1/60 grain per gallon) can also be used, but this drug can produce a

White Cloud Mountain Minnow infected with velvet disease. This species and other members of the carp family are particularly susceptible to the disease.

temporary sterility in fish. The original tank must also be sterilized and the plants removed and washed in a solution of potassium permanganate. The gravel should be washed and preferably left for ten minutes in boiling water. The water from the tank must be discarded and the inside well rinsed with a weak solution of a disinfectant detergent before a final rinse with fresh water. If this cleaning is not done further outbreaks of velvet will continually occur in the infected tank. The cure should be effective in a few days but a second treatment can be repeated in five or six days.

We believe that every introduction of this disease into aquarists' tanks is from infected fish or from the water in which they were contained.

1

Costia

2

Chilodon

3

Ichthyophonus

Saprolegnia

4

Other diseases and enemies

Costiasis is caused by a protozoan parasite *Costia necatrix* which grows in the mucus on the skin of fish. The fish become very lethargic with no appetite and respire rapidly. Fish can be cured by putting them in a two-and-a-half percent salt water solution for 15 minutes every day.

The protozoan *Chilodon cyprini* attaches itself to both the gills and skin of the fish. The fish closes its dorsal and anal fins and often spirals up to the surface to grasp a bubble of air. Methylene blue or acriflavin are cures.

Ichthyophonus hoferi is a widely distributed species of fungi and probably the cause of many unidentified deaths in fish. The illustration shows a section through a cyst from a fish's liver. The fungus grows through the intestinal lining and throughout the body. All fish suspected of infection should be removed and destroyed.

Saprolegnia fungi are present in all aquariums but only attack fish when skin damage has occurred. The parasite grows at the wound and produces a cotton wool-like growth, but mycelia will eventually invade the body tissues. Contaminated fish should be removed and the wound painted daily with a five percent methylene blue solution until healed.

Columnaris disease is caused by a bacterial infection *Chondococus columnaris*. This usually enters the body through injured areas, generally near the mouth and a fungus-like growth develops. One 250 mg capsule of chloramphenicol per gallon usually effects a cure.

Fin rot is a bacterial infection of the fins. Entry is gained through a damaged fin and inflammation and destruction of fin tissues takes place. The disease can spread into the body and result in death. A weak solution of acriflavin or penicillin (1/60 grain per gallon) is an effective cure.

Pop-eye exophthalmos is commonly seen in Siamese Fighting Fish. One eye becomes cloudy, swells and will lose its sight if not treated. The fish should be put in a net and one drop of organic silver eye drops applied four times a day.

Fluke infections are caused by trematode worms. Of these, *Gyrodactylus* species grow on the body and *Dactylogyrus* species on the gills. An infected fish becomes pale, with wide open pale gills

Columnaris

5

6

Fin rot

Pop-eye

7

Fluke infection

8

Humpy back

Air bladder disease

Dropsy

Shock

and torn and slimy fins. The fish should be kept in a deep blue solution of methylene blue for three days.

Senile changes occur in fish just as in other animals when they become old. They become incapable of breeding, often lose a lot of their color and develop deformities. A humpy back and air bladder disease are common among old fish. Air bladder disease causes the fish to lose its ability to balance. It is suggested that infection, incorrect feeding, indigestion and low water temperatures can cause this trouble.

Dropsy is a disease in which the cavities of the body accumulate fluids until the scales tend to stick out at right angles. There is evidence that this is a virus infection but 250 mg of chloramphenicol per gallon added to the water will usually cure. When only a single fish develops this disease, it does not normally spread.

Fish are vulnerable to sudden shocks. If tetras, for example, are transferred from acid to hard alkaline water they will turn over and perhaps die. Fish placed in water of a different temperature will also show shock symptoms and fish chased by the net when being caught may roll over on their backs and look very ill.

Among the enemies of fish are hydras, small coelenterates living in freshwater ponds. They feed mainly on water fleas which they first paralyze and then ingest. Hydras are quite capable of killing small fish up to half an inch long. If a tank gets infected with hydras a few guppies or gouramies will soon clear them up if they are given no other food.

The Great Diving Beetle (*Dytiscus marginalis*) is present in many of the ponds which contain water fleas and therefore its larval form is likely to be caught in catches of *Daphnia*. The larva has large jaws through which it injects digestive juices before sucking up its victims' tissues. It can kill fish larger than itself using this method.

Dragonflies lay their eggs in water and the larvae are very voracious and will kill fish larger than themselves. Any caught with *Daphnia* should be removed.

Piscicola geomatra is a fresh-water leech that will attack fish. Other leeches found in ponds will attack only mammals, amphibians or snails.

Hydras

Great Diving Beetle

Dragonfly larva

Piscicola

137

Sediment settles out down the slope of the gravel

SETTING UP THE HOME AQUARIUM

Setting up an aquarium in the home must be a carefully thought out operation. First of all, thought must be given to where the tank is to go, remembering weight, size, amount of daylight and so on. Tanks to be built into alcoves need even more thought. There should be enough room above the tank for servicing, and the tank should be capable of being moved fairly easily if necessary. A plug for the electricity supply to carry heater, thermostats, lighting, and provision for working an air pump is needed. Electricity and water are a dangerous combination, so all electrical work should be done properly. It is also a good idea to conceal wires, connections and plugs or these will detract from the appearance of the tank.

Cost must obviously determine tank size but for a community tank 24 inches × 12 inches × 12 inches is the minimum size for setting up an 'aquascape'. It is well worth spending extra money on the tank and equipment in the beginning, as fish can be gradually added later. Second-hand tanks should be bought with care, particularly if they have been stored dry for a considerable length of time. They tend to leak when filled with water and leaks are difficult to stop. Nevertheless, all tanks, whether new or second-hand should be put outside, filled with water and left for one week as a test. This week can be utilized for preliminary tasks, such as the preparation of the gravel. All aquarium composts, no matter how well washed they are reputed to be, always need additional washing.

When gravel is put into the tank, it must always slope from back to front to allow detritus and sediment to settle to the front glass, from where it is easy to siphon off (see page 146).

Before adding the water it is advisable to place a layer of newspaper on the gravel. This prevents the water from disturb-

Flow diagram to show stages in setting up an aquarium

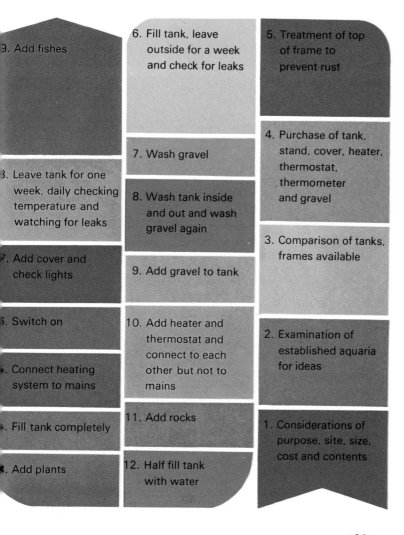

9. Add fishes

6. Fill tank, leave outside for a week and check for leaks

5. Treatment of top of frame to prevent rust

7. Wash gravel

4. Purchase of tank, stand, cover, heater, thermostat, thermometer and gravel

8. Leave tank for one week, daily checking temperature and watching for leaks

8. Wash tank inside and out and wash gravel again

3. Comparison of tanks, frames available

7. Add cover and check lights

9. Add gravel to tank

6. Switch on

10. Add heater and thermostat and connect to each other but not to mains

2. Examination of established aquaria for ideas

5. Connect heating system to mains

4. Fill tank completely

11. Add rocks

1. Considerations of purpose, site, size, cost and contents

3. Add plants

12. Half fill tank with water

Add the water carefully over newspaper to avoid distubing the gravel

ing the gravel and causing clouding. Water should be added at about 70° F, and when the tank is half full the rocks can be added. Rocks composed of limestone and marble should not be used as these will make the water very alkaline and cloudy. Granite and sandstone are very good rocks for aquaria, but they must be well washed before they are placed in the tank.

Rockwork can be bought at pet shops, artificial rockwork can be made out of concrete or the aquarist can collect natural

Red shale makes attractive aquarium rockwork

rocks for his aquarium. There is no doubt that the latter produce the most beautiful effect. Concrete 'rockwork' must be well cured before use in the aquarium or the water is made very alkaline and will harm the fish. The shape, size and color of the rock placed in the tank depends on the artistic abilities of the aquarist, but it must blend in with the gravel and plants. Generally, tall pieces are placed at the back and small pieces at the front.

The heater and thermostat are placed at opposite corners of the tank, the heater inclined at an angle and the thermostat vertical. If these two are placed near each other, cold pockets in the aquarium will be produced. There are very often layers of different temperatures in the aquarium, the bottom being a few degrees cooler than the surface. This is due somewhat to the bulb lighting the aquarium as this also heats the surface of the water. The thermometer is best positioned on the front glass on the same side as the thermostat, with its bulb in the middle of the tank.

Small fluctuations in temperature will not harm the fish; in fact a slightly varying temperature is preferable to an exactly constant one. However, sudden changes will result in loss of fish, and once the tank is set up it is wise to check the temperature daily.

Thermostat and heater positions for even temperature

Suggested plan (*above*) and side view showing species (*opposite*) of a community tank planting. Species are *Ech. paniculatus* (1); *Crypt.*

Plants are best added to the aquarium when it is only half full of water. Planting sticks may be used and are a great help when putting in the last few plants. It is advisable not to lead down plants as lead in soft water produces lead hydroxide, which is poisonous. The plant roots should be pushed into the gravel as deep as the crown of the plant but must be handled delicately. The variety of plants used and how many, depends upon the taste of the aquarist. It is important not to over-plant because the plants will grow and over-crowding will result.

For community tanks some aquarists prefer mixtures of cryptocorynes with a little *Sagittaria* but others have different preferences. Plants like Indian fern and Giant Hygrophila often grow extremely fast, but cryptocorynes grow slowly so that a reasonably stable environment is presented. Floating plants do very poorly in the community aquarium indoors because heat from the electric light bulbs in the tank cover scorch them. As they also block light from the other plants, they really have no place in the indoor community tank.

Once all the plants are in, the tank can be completely filled. It is advisable to do this by using a watering can with a rose attachment. An occasional plant may float during this procedure but can be replanted with planting sticks without too *affinis* (2); *Crypt. becketti* (3); *Cabomba* (4); *Bacopa* (5); *Crypt. nevelli* (6); and *Ech. tenellis* (7).

much difficulty. It takes a little time for the plants to establish themselves and the week allowed to stablize temperatures and check leaks before the fish are put in gives the plants time to settle down and begin to root. During early stages of the life of a new tank, algae may appear as they have at this stage no competition from the higher plants. This algae is best controlled by temporarily cutting down the light.

Razor blade glass scraper (*top*) and planting stick (*bottom*)

Suggested guide to the surface area requirements of fish based on their ultimate size

Fish	Maximum size (ins.)	Surface area required per fish (sq. in.)
guppy	2	5
neon	2	5
swordtail	3	20
platy	3	20
fighter	3	20
Gyrinocheilus	3	20
barb	3½	30
cichlid	5	60

For example, a 24-inch × 12-inch × 12-inch tank (surface area 288 sq. inches) would hold, assuming they were of maximum size, six guppies, one angel, six swordtails, two barbs and one *Gyrinocheilus* —a total surface area requirement of 290 sq. inches.

Once the tank has been working properly for a week, the fish can be bought. The selection depends upon the taste of the aquarist, but for a complete beginner fish should be selected from the following species: guppies, swordtails, platies, smaller barbs, mollies, tetras, Zebra Danios and one *Gyrinocheilus aymonieri*. These are all colorful fish and will live together peacefully. One male Siamese Fighting Fish can be added to provide a dash of color and will probably become a conversation piece. Angelfish, if added, should be fairly small because large specimens may eat other fish. It is always better to have more than one fish of a species as they then act as a stimulus to each other and their coloring is shown off to best advantage. Another way to stock a community aquarium is with fish of one species only. This can produce wonderful effects, especially with schooling species.

It is very important not to overcrowd the aquarium as this leads to poor-looking fish and a tendency toward disease. It is well to remember that fish bought at pet shops are usually young and will grow larger in a tank.

When buying fish, it is important to choose healthy specimens and to transport them home carefully. It is a good idea to make a small carrying case lined with expanded styrofoam in which the bag of fish can be transported without loss of heat. For journeys of up to four hours the air above the water in the bag will be sufficient for the fish, but for a longer journey the bag is better filled with oxygen. All large fish dealers will pack your fish when a long journey home is involved. Once home, the fish must be carefully transferred to the tank, but preferably first to a quarantine tank.

They are best introduced by first floating the sealed bag in the aquarium to allow its temperature to adjust to that of the tank. The bag can then be opened and a small amount of tank water introduced. If no ill effects are apparent, tank water can be introduced every half hour, until the water in the bag is nearly all tank water. The bag should then be allowed to sink in the tank and fish gently turned out. This prevents shock that might otherwise be caused by changes in pH, hardness, osmotic pressure and temperature. Once released, the fish should be given a small amount of some tempting live food to help introduce them to their new home.

An insulated carrying case is useful for transporting tropical fish

Sediment can be removed by siphon but the water must be replaced, of course. The apparatus below removes debris without drawing off any water.

A tropical fish tank needs very little maintenance. Water evaporates and has to be replaced, theoretically with distilled water but in practice tap water will do. About once every month sufficient sediment will have collected on the gravel to spoil its clean appearance and this should be siphoned off with a siphon tube. A piece of clear plastic tube about ¾-inch in diameter is useful for this. In running the siphon, six gallons of water are usually taken out and replaced by fresh water.

The only other occasional job for the aquarist is to scrape off the algae growing on the ·glass of his aquarium. Only the front glass needs to be cleaned regularly, for algal growths on the back and sides can be beneficial. Algae are good oxygenators and prevent strong light entering

heavier particles settle out in lower rate of flow

water and sediment drawn up by air lift

the tank from the sides. Removal is easily done with a razor blade scraper, though this job is done very effectively by the fish *Gryinocheilus aymonieri,* one of which should be included in every community tank for this purpose.

Each day, when feeding his fish, the aquarist should feel the temperature of the tank with the back of his fingers. In this way he will soon become experienced at estimating tank temperatures and this is very useful. Thermometers can go wrong, heaters can break and thermostats can stick, so a daily check on the temperature by themometer and hand is a useful routine.

The only other danger, other than introducing diseased fish or predators into the tank, is over-feeding. This danger cannot be stressed enough to the novice fish keeper. When the aquarist goes on a vacation, the fish are much better off if not fed for up to three weeks in preference to having some novice fish keeper overfeeding them. Excess food in the tank will rot and cause a relative lack of oxygen which kills the fish.

Gyrinocheilus aymonieri is a useful aquarium fish. It cleans algae not only from aquarium glass but from the plants as well.

An attractive display of coral in a marine aquarium

The tropical marine aquarium

A number of tropical freshwater aquarists graduate to keeping tropical marine aquaria. These are much more difficult to keep. The tank must be all glass or all plastic, as sea water attacks metals releasing toxic metal ions which will kill the fish. Sea water is difficult to acquire unless one lives at the coast and even then it has to be taken from well out at sea to avoid pollution from rivers and sewage. Salts for preparing artificial sea water are now available, however. The tank must be equipped with efficient filtration and aeration systems. The loss of water by evaporation must be made up with distilled water and the density checked with a hydrometer. The bottom should be covered with washed silver sand and although there is no seaweed that will flourish in an aquarium, attractive displays can be made up with different varieties of corals and shells. Coral should be boiled before being placed in the aquarium.

Feeding can be a problem, as most coral fish are carnivorous and will not take dried food. They can be fed *Daphnia*, *Tubifex*, whiteworm and small freshwater fish. None of these foods lives long in salt water and therefore once they are dead must be quickly removed to prevent pollution. Adult Brine Shrimp are suitable, but special arrangements have to be made to rear these to adult size.

Tropical marine fish

The Clown Anemone Fish (*Amphiprion percula*) is a native of the Indian Ocean and southeast Asia. It has an interesting relationship with anemones of the genera *Stoichactis* and *Dicosoma*. The Clown Fish are immune to the poisonous tentacles of the anemone among which they hide for protection.

The Pygmy Sea Horse (*Hippocampus zosterae*) is a fish in spite of its name and appearance. It has a prehensile tail, and the male broods the eggs. Many of the public Aquaria have good displays of these or other species of sea horse.

The Moorish Idol (*Zanclus canescens*) is probably the most coveted of all coral fish but one of the most difficult to keep alive.

The Neon Goby (*Elacatinus oceanops*) is a very beautiful, active fish. It is noted for its habit of cleaning external parasites from other larger fish.

The Emperor Angelfish (*Pomacanthus imperator*) is a hardy fish, but has a tendency to be aggressive with its own and similar species.

Clown Anemone Fish (1); Pygmy Sea Horse (2); Moorish Idol (3); Neon Goby (4); Emperor Angelfish (5)

Showing fish

Fish shows may take the form of competitions between two or more fish clubs, or large, open shows where fish are entered by individuals from all over. The larger shows are usually advertised in aquatic journals and are well worth a visit by the beginner as large numbers of excellent fish are generally on display and occasionally for sale.

In all large aquarium shows there is usually a furnished aquarium section. Here the competitor is required to set up a complete aquatic landscape—generally in a standard-sized tank—and the judge usually gives marks according to the following criteria: design and character; fish and plants (their selection, quality and condition); and technique. Often there are separate classes for individual families of fish, for example, live bearers, carp, barbs, minnows, cichlids, labyrinths and a final group covering any other variety. Specific show standards have been set for many different kinds of fish, and the aquarist wishing to participate in any competitive exhibition should be aware of the criteria set for the kind of fish he is interested in showing.

The standard methods of judging that are generally used give marks for condition and style of fish, color of fish, and relative size of fish. In some cases lists are published which

Show standard of *Betta splendens*

show, for example, the size of swordtail that would receive the full point score and the relative score for smaller or less perfect ones. In allocation of marks for color, style and condition, the judge has to rely on his experience.

In areas where frequent large exhibitions are not feasible, some local aquarium societies have started household aquarium competitions. In these, a committee composed of a few members of the society visit aquariums at the homes of the owners. One judging system used in such competitions is as follows:

Aquarium (design, appearance, location)	25 pts.
Fish (condition and beauty of individuals)	25 pts.
Plants (arrangement, condition, varieties—all must be in growing condition)	40 pts.
General appearance	10 pts.
	100 pts.

Competition in most aquarium shows is limited to the amateur aquarist, but some shows do have special awards for dealers and professional breeders. Sometimes shows also include a competition for home-made aquariums. These must be working aquariums and contain plants and fish, but the award is given for excellence of workmanship on the tank.

Example of a judge's scoring card

No. of tank *16*

	Total marks possible	Marks awarded
Plant and accessory arrangement........	20	*18*
Variety and rarity of fish.............	20	*19*
Variety of plant material..............	15	*12*
General artistic effect................	15	*13*
Aquarium design........................	10	*8*
Quality of plant material..............	10	*8*
Other aquatic fauna....................	10	*6*
	100	*84*

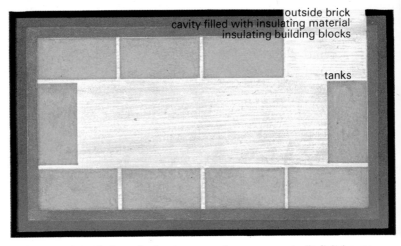

outside brick
cavity filled with insulating material
insulating building blocks

tanks

Floor and roof plan of a large, expensive, purpose-built fish house

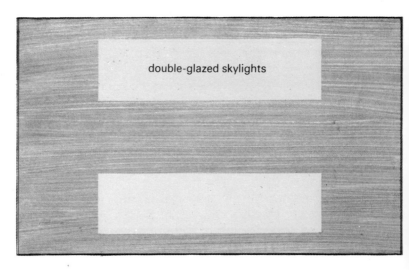

double-glazed skylights

Fish houses and fish rooms

Many aquarists eventually get to the stage when they need a special place for their fish tanks. In the special fish house the design can be purely functional, bearing in mind the needs of the aquarist. If he wants to grow plants as well as fish, for example, provision must be made for more natural light. Whether he decides to heat individual tanks or space heat the whole fish house will depend largely at what temperature he likes to work. Greenhouses on the whole make poor fish houses as they get too warm in summer, lose too much heat in winter and allow too much natural light to enter, causing an overgrowth of algae.

In the more common type of fish house, where tanks line one or more walls but the room contains sofas, relaxing chairs and so on the design can obviously not be as functional. Whatever the type of aquarium accommodation, conservation of heat by double-glazing of windows, building with insulating blocks, cavity walls filled with polyurethane foams and so on are all very helpful and are to be recommended.

Aquarium societies

Aquarium societies exist at international, national and local levels, and the local aquarium society is by far the most valuable. Larger local societies often have a speaker from outside the club who gives a talk on his special subject, followed by discussion. Many local clubs also hold small exhibitions either between club members or, from time to time, with other local clubs. In addition to these activities there is the opportunity of meeting and talking with other local aquarists. Some clubs also organize outings to dealers and other places of aquatic interest.

Some of the larger clubs organize conventions, occasionally bringing distinguished speakers from other countries. They have also arranged large open shows and competitions.

Fish collection

Today, many of the more common tropical fish found in home aquaria are bred by wholesale dealers. Many of these are to be found in the southern half of the country where the weather is milder and heating expenses are lower. These fish are then shipped to wholesale sellers and from there to local pet shops.

Many fish that cannot be easily bred in the aquarium are collected in the wild in tropical areas of the world and shipped to the United States. Years ago the only way for a would-be collector to acquire tropical fish would be for that individual to travel to a warm-climate area and bring back the desired species. Today, however, there exists a large network of native collectors and local distributors throughout the tropical world, bringing fish directly to northern markets.

Collectors are also always on the look-out for new species. Once the fish are caught, transportation is often difficult, especially if the collector has had to go far into the bush to find his specimens. On arrival at a central base, the fish are inspected and sorted and great care is taken with them by the collector until they are sold to a dealer — the second stage of their journey to the home tanks. Finally they are put into large, double plastic bags which are filled with water and then blown up with oxygen to further guarantee the safe arrival of the fish. Small amounts of a drug called sodium amytol are put into the water; it tends to slow down all the fish's body processes. The bags are then placed in insulated boxes and flown to their destination. They are collected by dealers on arrival and placed in quarantine tanks before resale to aquarists.

Pet shops and fish dealers

Pet shops and dealers become very important to the aquarist and each soon has his favorite shop. Most towns have a local pet shop which keeps and sells all sorts of pets and pet foods and has anything from two to a hundred tanks of tropical fish. This type of pet shop usually stocks all aquarium equipment and foods. Such local shops often tend to be a meeting place for local aquarists who are found standing around talking and watching if not actually buying. This type of shop buys fish from wholesalers or from aquarists whenever they have surplus stock.

The commercial fish breeder, often with large fish houses, breeds many varieties himself and often imports fish from the tropics or from importers in Germany or Holland. Many of these dealers are naturally aquarists with great experience in fish breeding and fish keeping. Many of them sell both wholesale and retail.

Individual aquarists or aquarist societies are welcome by appointment at many of these establishments. In areas where the weather is warm, large commercial fish farms exist where the breeding and rearing of large numbers of tropical fish takes place in outdoor pools and tanks.

Large fish farm in southern United States

BOOKS TO READ

The Complete Aquarist's Guide to Freshwater Tropical Fishes. Golden Press, 1970.

Encyclopedia of Tropical Fishes. H.R. Axelrod and W. Vorderwinkler. T.F.H. Publications, 1966.

Illustrated Dictionary of Tropical Fishes. H. Frey. T.F.H. Publications, 1961.

Tropical Aquarium Fish — Their Habits and Breeding Behavior. A. Nieuwenhuizen. Van Nostrand, 1964.

Tropical Fish as Pets. C.W. Coates. New York: Liveright, 1950.

Tropical Fish as a Hobby. H.R. Axelrod. McGraw-Hill, 1969.

Fishes of the World. Allan Cooper. Grosset & Dunlap, 1971.

Exotic Tropical Fishes. H.R. Axelrod *et al.* T.F.H. Publications, 1962.

Exotic Aquarium Fish. W.T. Innes. T.F.H. Publications, 1968.

Freshwater Tropical Aquarium Fishes. G.F. Hervey and J. Hems. London: Spring Books, 1965.

Breeding Aquarium Fishes. H.R. Axelrod and S. Shaw. T.F.H. Publications, 1962.

Field Book of Marine Fishes of the Atlantic Coast. C.M. Breder, Jr. G.P. Putnam's Sons, 1948.

The Captive Sea. C. Phillips. Philadelphia: Chilton Books, 1964.

The Fishes. Life Nature Library. Time-Life, 1969.

Living Fishes of the World. Earl S. Herald. Doubleday.

The following journals are also of interest to the aquarist:

Tropical Fish Hobbyist
The Aquarium Magazine
The Aquarist and Pondkeeper (British)
Pet Fish Monthly (British)

PLACES TO VISIT

New York Aquarium, Brooklyn, New York
Shedd Aquarium, Chicago, Illinois
Marineland, San Diego, California
Steinhart Aquarium, San Francisco, California
Cleveland Aquarium, Cleveland, Ohio
Municipal Aquarium, Key West, Florida

NDEX

age numbers in bold type
efer to illustrations

*canthodoras spinosis-
   simus* 112, **112**
canthophthalmus kuhlii
   114, **114**
corus 33, **33**
equidens sp 107, **107**
.frican Knifefish 117, **117**
.gassiz's Dwarf Cichlid
   106, **106**
ir bladder disease 136,
   136
ir pumps 25, **25,**138
lgae 21, **21,** 59, 60, 112,
   113, 120, 143, 146
mazon Swordplant 37, **37**
mblyopsis spelaeus 63,
   63
mphiprion percula 149,
   149
nabantidae 82–89
nabas testudineus 86, **86**
nableps anableps 63, **63**
ngelfish **110,** 111, 144
nguilluda silusia 127, **127**
phyocypris pooni 73, **73**
physemion sp 18, **27,**
   66, **67, 69**
pistogramma sp 106, **106**
plocheilus lineatus 66, **67**
ponogeton sp 38–39, **38**
quarium societies 153
quarium equipment
   20–27
quascapes 11, 138
rapaima gigas 7, **7,** 119
rcherfish 117, **117**
rtemia salina 127, **127**
stronotus ocellatus 107,
   107
ustralian Rainbowfish 44
zolla 40, **40**

acopa 33, **33, 143**
anded Cichlid 108, **108**
arbodes sp 76, **76**
arbs 75–81, 144
   breeding 79–81
arbus tor 70
eacon Fish 94, **94,**101
edotia geayi 18
elonesox belizanus 61, **62**
elontia signata 86, **86**
entos Tetra 93, **93**
erlin Swordtail 59, **59**
etta sp 83, **83, 84, 85,**
   86, **86,** 135, 144
ack-banded Sunfish 115,
   115
ack-line Tetra 101
ack Neon 93, **93**
ack Ruby Barb 77, **77**
ack Sail-fin Molly **56,**
   56–57, **130**

Black Widow 100
Bleeding Heart Tetra 92, **92**
Blindfish 63, **63**
Bloodworms 125, **125**
Blue Acara 107, **107**
Blue Gularis **69**
Bog plants **11,** 30–31, **31,**
   36
Botia macrocanthus 114,
   114
Brachydanio sp 72, **72,** 78,
   78
Brachygobius xanthozona
   117, **117**
Breeding mop 65, **65, 80,**
   81, 102, **102**
Breeding traps 53, **53,** 63,
   80
Brine Shrimp 127, **127,** 148
Bronze Catfish 112, **112**
Bumblebee-fish 117, **117**
Butterfly-fish 116, **116**

Cabomba 39, **39, 143**
Capoeta sp 46, **70,** 75,
   75, 76, **76,** 77, **77,** 78
Carassius auratus 70–71,
   70 71
Cardinal Tetra 91, **91**
Carrying case 144, **145**
Celebes Sailfin 18
Celestial Goldfish 71
Cellophane plant 36, **36**
Ceratopteris 40, **40**
Chain Swordplant 37, **37**
Chanda lala 116, **116**
Characidae 90–103
   breeding 100–103
Cheirodon axelrodi 91, **91**
Chequered Barb 76, **76**
Cherry Barb 77, **77, 78**
Chilodon cyprini 134, **134**
Chocolate Gourami 89, **89**
Chorynopoma riisei 97, **97**
Cichlasoma sp 44, 107,
   107, 108, **108**
Cichlidae 104–111
   breeding 104–105, **105**
Classification of fish
   46–49, **48–49**
Climbing Perch 86, **86**
Clown Anemone Fish 149,
   149
Clown Loach 114, **114**
Colisa sp 7, 86, **86,** 88, **88**
Columnaris 135, **135**
Comb-tail Paradise Fish 86,
   86
Comet Goldfish **70,** 71
Common Puffer-fish 117,
   117
Composts 20, **20,** 25,
   138–139
Congenital diseases 128
Congo Tetra 99, **99**
Copeina arnoldi 96, **96**

Corydoras aeneus 112, **112**
Costiasis 134, **134**
Covers 26–27, **26**
Crenicichla lepidota 108,
   108
Cryptocoryne sp 18, **31,**
   34–35, **34–35,** 142, **143**
Crystalwort 41, **41**
Cyclops 124, **124**
Cynolebias nigripinnis 68,
   69
Cyprinidae 70–81, 132
Cyprinodontidae 64–69

Danios 72, **72**
   breeding 79–81
Danio malabaricus 72, **72**
Daphnia 120, 124, **124,**
   133, 137, 148
Degenerative diseases 129
Dermogenys pusillus 63, **63**
Discus **110,** 111
Diseases of fish 128–137
Dragonfly larvae 137, **137**
Dried foods 120–121
Dropsy 136, **136**
Duckweed 40, **40**
Dwarf Argentine Pearlfish
   68, **69**
Dwarf Gourami 88, **88**
Dwarf Rainbowfish 114,
   115
Dwarf Top Minnow 62, **62**
Dytiscus marginalis 137,
   137

Earthworm 120
Echinodorus sp 36–37,
   36–37, 143
Eggfish 71, **71**
Egg-laying tooth-carps 30,
   44, 64–69
   egg-buriers 64, 68–69, **69**
   egg-hangers 64–67
Eichornia crassipes 40, **40**
Elacatinus oceanops 149,
   149
Electric Catfish 119, **119**
Emperor Angelfish 149, **149**
Emperor Tetra 99, **99**
Enchytraeus sp **122,** 123,
   127
Epiplatys chaperi 66, **67**
Etroplus maculatus 109, **109**
Evolution of fish **42,** 43
Eye-spot Rasbora **74**

Fairy moss 40, **40**
Feeding 120–129, 147, 148
Fiberglas aquarium 13
Filtration 25
Fin rot 135, **135**
Fire-mouth Cichlid 44, 108,
   108
Fire-mouth Panchax 66, **67**
Fish houses 152–153, **152**

Flame Tetra 93, **93**
Floating fern 40
Fluke infections 135, **135**
Freshwater Shrimp 125, **125**

Gambusia sp **46**, 62, **62**
Gammarus pulex 125, **125**
Geophagus sp 104, 108, **108**
Giant Danio 72, **72**
Giant Gourami 7
Giant Hygrophila 142
Giant Sail-fin Molly 57, **57**
Glass aquarium 13
Glass Catfish 113, **113**
Glassfish 116, **116**
Glass larvae 125, **125**
Glowlight Tetra 95, **95**, 103, **103**
Gnat larvae 124, **125**
Golden Barb 76
Golden Double Sword Guppy 55, **55**
Golden-eyed Dwarf Cichlid 106, **106**
Golden Pheasant **69**
Golden Wagtail **60**
Goldfish 70–71, **70–71**
Gonopodium 50, 51, **51**, 62
Gourami **7**, **82**, 137
Great Diving Beetle 137, **137**
Green Lace Guppy 54, **54**
Green Swordtail 58, **58**
Grindal worms 127
Guppy 54–55, **54–55**, 137, 144
Gymnocorymbus ternetzi 100
Gyrinocheilus aymonieri 114, **114**, 144, 147, **147**

Half-beak 63, **63**
Half-banded Barb 76, **76**
Haplochromis multicolor 109, **109**
Hardness of water 18
Harlequin Fish 74, **74**
Head-and- Tail-Light Fish 94, **94**
Heaters 23, **23**, 138, 141, **141**
Helostoma temmincki 89, **89**
Hemichromis bimaculatus 109, **109**
Hemigrammus sp 94, **94**, 95, **95**, 101
Heterandria formosa **46**, 62, **62**
Hippocampus zosterae 149, **149**
Honey Gourami 86, **86**
Hump-back Limia 63, **63**
Humpy back **45**, 136, **136**
Hydra 137, **137**
Hygrophila polysperma 39, **39**
Hyphessobrycon sp 91, 92, **92**, 93, **93**, 101, **101**

Ichthyophonus hoferi 134, **134**
Ichthyophthirius multifilius 130–131. **130**, **131**
Indian Fern 40, 52, 142
Infectious diseases 128–129
Infusoria 52, 126, **126**

Jack Dempsey 107, **107**
'Japanese Rush' 33, **33**
Javan Mouth-breeding Fighting Fish 86, **86**
Jenynsia lineata 62, **62**

Keyhole Cichlid 107, **107**
Kissing Gourami 89, **89**
Kryptopterus bicirrhis 113, **113**
Kuhli Loach 114, **114**

Labyrinth fish 82–89, 132
Labyrinth organ 82, **82**, 86
Lebistes reticulatus 54–55, **54–55**
Leeches 137, **137**
Lemna 40, **40**
Lemon Tetra 92, **92**
Leopard Danio 72, **78**
Lighting 21, **21**, 31, 138
Limnia nigrofasciata 63, **63**
Lionhead Goldfish 71, **71**
Live-bearing tooth-carps 50–63
    breeding 52–53
Loricaria parva 112, **112**
Ludwigia natans 39, **39**
Lungfish 118, **118**

Macropodus opercularis 4, 87, **87**
Madagascar Lace plant 38, **38**
Malapterurus electricus 119, **119**
Malayan Angel 115, **115**
Marbled Cichlid 107, **107**
Marine aquarium 148–149, **148**
Mastacembelus maculatus 116, **116**
Melanotaenia sp 44, 114, **115**
Mesogonistius chaetodon 115, **115**
Methylene blue 130–131, 133, 134, 135
Metynnis schreitmuelleri 98, **98**
Micro-worm 127, **127**
Minnow 70, **70**
Mollienesia sp 56–57, **56**, **57**
Mollies 56–57, **56–57**, 144
Monodactylus argenteus 115, **115**
Moorish Idol 149, **149**
Mosquito Fish 46, 62, **62**
Mozambique Cichlid 109, **109**
Mudskipper 116, **116**
Myriophyllum 39, **39**, 52

Najas 41, **41**
Nannacara anomala 106, **106**
Nannastomus anomalus 99, **99**
Nematobrycon palmeri 99, **99**
Neolebias ansorgei 99, **99**
Neomacheilus fasciatus 114, **114**
Neon Goby 149, **149**
Neon Tetra 91, 101, **101**
Nomaphila stricta 39, **39**
Nothobranchius palmquist **69**

One-sided live-bearer 62, **6**
Oodinium limneticum 133
Orange Chromide 109, **10**
Osphronemus goramy **82**
Otocinclus vittatus 113, **1**
Oxygen supply 14–15, 22, 25

Pachypanchax playfairi 66, **67**
Pearl Danio 72, **72**
Pearl Gourami 89, **89**
Pelmatochromis kirbensis 106, **106**
Periophthalmus barbarus 116, **116**
pH of water 19, **19**
Phenocogrammus inter-ruptus 99, **99**
Phoxinus phoxinus 70, **70**
Physical structure of fish 44–45, **44–45**
Pike Cichlid 108, **108**
Pike Top Minnow 61, **62**
Pimelodella gracilis 112, **112**
Piscicola geomatra 137, **13**
Pistia 41, **41**
Planting sticks 142, **143**
Plants 14, 18, 20, 21, 30–41, 52, 120, 142–143, **142**, **143**
Plastic aquarium **12**, 13
Platy 18, **46**, 59–61, **60–61**, 144
Plecostomus commersoni 113, **113**, 114
Plistophora 91
Poeciliidae 50–63
Pomacanthus imperator 149, **149**
Pop-eye 135, **135**
Pristella riddlei 98, **98**
Pterois volitans **11**
Pterophyllum sp 18, **110**, 111
Public Aquaria 4, 6–7, **6**, 118, 149
Puntius sp 77, **77**
Pygmy Sea Horse 149, **149**

Quarantine tank 129, 145

Ramirez' Dwarf Cichlid
  106, **106**
Rasbora sp 74, **74,** 75
Razor blade scraper **143,**
  147
Red Cichlid 109, **109**
Red-eyed Swordtail **58,** 59
Red Piranha 98, **98**
Red Platy **61**
Red Ramshorn 29, **29**
Red Tetra 93, **93**
Red Wagtail Swordtail **58,**
  59
Riccia 41, **41,** 52
Rivulus cylindraceus 66, **67**
Rocks 140–141, **140**
Roloffia occidentalis **69**
Rooseveltiella nattereri 98,
  98
Rosy Barb 77, **77**
Rosy Tetra 92, **92**

Sagittaria sp 33, **33,** 142
Sail-fin Molly 18, **56,** 57
Salvinia 41, **41**
Saprolegnia 134, **134**
Scarf-tail Guppy 54, **54**
Scat 115, **115**
Scatophagus argus 115, **115**
Scissor-tail Rasbora 75
Senile changes 136, **136**
Serrasalmus rhombeus 98,
  98
Shock 136, **136**
Showing fish 150–151
Show standards 150–151
Shubunkin 71, **71**
Siamese Fighting Fish 83,
  83, 84, 85, 135, 144, **150**
  breeding 84–85, **85**

'Simpson Swordtail' 59, **59**
Small Mouth-breeder 109,
  109
Snails 28–29, **29**
*Sphaerichthys osphromen-
  oides* 89, **89**
Spiny Catfish 112, **112**
Spiny Eel 116, **116**
Spotted Danio 72, **72**
Spotted Rasbora **74,** 75
Spraying Characin 96, **96**
Stand, for aquarium 8, **9, 10**
Steel angle **9,** 10
Swordtail Characin 97, **97**
Swordtails 46, 51, 58–59,
  58–59, 144
Symphysodon discus 18,
  110, 111
Synodontis nigriventris 113,
  113

Tanichthys albonubes 18,
  73, **73**
Telescope Veiltail Goldfish
  71
Telmatherina ladigesi 18
Temperature 10, 22, 24, 30,
  147
Tetraodon cutcutia 117,
  117
Tetras 144
Thermometer 22, **22**
Thermostats 24, **24,** 138,
  141, **141**
Three-spot Gourami 89, **89**
Tiger Barb 46, **70,** 75, **75**
Tilapia sp 5, 104
  mossambica 109, **109**
Tinfoil Barb 76, **76**
Toxotes jaculator 117, **117**

Traumatic diseases 128
Trichogaster sp 89, **89**
Tubifex 120, **122,** 123, 148
Two-spot Barb 77, **77**

Upside-down Catfish 113,
  113

Vallisneria sp 32, **32**
Variegated Platy 60–61, **61**
Veiltail Goldfish 71, **71**
Veiltail Guppy 55, **55**
Velvet disease 132–133,
  132, 133

Water 10
Water cycle 16–17, **16–17**
Water Hyacinth 40, **40**
Water Lettuce 41, **41**
Water Milfoil 39, **39**
Whiptail Catfish 112, **112**
White Cloud Mountain
  Minnow 73, **73,** 132, **133**
White Piranha 98, **98**
White spot disease
  130–131, **130, 131**
Whiteworm 120, **122,** 123,
  148

Xenomystus nigri 117, **117**
Xiphophorus sp 46, 58,
  58, 60–61, **61**
X-ray Fish 98, **98**

Zanclus canescens 149, **149**
Zebra Danio 72, **72, 78,**
  102, 144

OTHER TITLES IN THE SERIES

The GROSSET ALL-COLOR GUIDES provide a library of authoritative information for readers of all ages. Each comprehensive text with its specially designed illustrations yields a unique insight into a particular area of man's interests and culture.

NOW AVAILABLE

PREHISTORIC ANIMALS
BIRD BEHAVIOR
WILD CATS
FOSSIL MAN
PORCELAIN
MILITARY UNIFORMS 1686–1918
BIRDS OF PREY
FLOWER ARRANGING
MICROSCOPES & MICROSCOPIC LIFE
THE PLANT KINGDOM
ROCKETS & MISSILES
FLAGS OF THE WORLD
ATOMIC ENERGY
WEATHER & WEATHER FORECASTING
TRAINS
SAILING SHIPS & SAILING CRAFT
ELECTRONICS
MYTHS & LEGENDS OF ANCIENT GREECE
CATS, HISTORY—CARE—BREEDS
DISCOVERY OF AFRICA
HORSES & PONIES
FISHES OF THE WORLD
ASTRONOMY
SNAKES OF THE WORLD
DOGS, SELECTION—CARE—TRAINING
MAMMALS OF THE WORLD
VICTORIAN FURNITURE AND FURNISHINGS
MYTHS & LEGENDS OF ANCIENT EGYPT
COMPUTERS AT WORK
GUNS

SOON TO BE PUBLISHED

THE ANIMAL KINGDOM
WARSHIPS
EXPLORING THE PLANETS
TROPICAL FRESHWATER AQUARIA
THE HUMAN BODY
ARCHITECTURE
EVOLUTION OF LIFE
VETERAN AND VINTAGE CARS
ARMS AND ARMOR
MATHEMATICS
DISCOVERY OF NORTH AMERICA
NATURAL HISTORY COLLECTING
ARCHAEOLOGY
MONKEYS AND APES
AIRCRAFT
HOUSE PLANTS
MYTHS AND LEGENDS OF ANCIENT ROME
SEA BIRDS
JEWELRY
ELECTRICITY
ANIMALS OF AUSTRALIA AND NEW ZEALAND
GLASS
MYTHS AND LEGENDS OF THE SOUTH SEAS
BUTTERFLIES
DISCOVERY OF AUSTRALIA
DISCOVERY OF SOUTH AMERICA
TROPICAL BIRDS
ANTIQUE FURNITURE
MYTHS AND LEGENDS OF INDIA
ANIMALS OF SOUTH AND CENTRAL AMERICA